COMPLIMENTS OF

PROGRESSIVE
SAVINGS AND LOAN ASSOCIATION

"progress and savings go hand in hand"

MAIN OFFICE: 2121 W. MAIN, ALHAMBRA • 289-9141

BRANCHES: LONG BEACH • PASADENA • TARZANA
REDONDO BEACH • STUDIO CITY • WEST COVINA

BEVERLY HILLS

D0538595

Better Homes and Gardens®

FLOWER ARRANGING

BETTER HOMES AND GARDENS BOOKS
NEW YORK • DES MOINES

©Meredith Corporation, 1965. All Rights Reserved.
Printed in the United States of America.
First Edition. Fourth Printing, 1973.
Library of Congress Catalog Card Number: 65-2704
SBN: 696-00100-4

Contents

An arrangement of roses and Scotch broom in a black lacquer container was designed by Flower Master Sofu Teshigahara, founder of the Sogetsu school of flower arranging.

Introduction

"Something remarkable has been happening during the past decade or two. The art of flower arranging, by no means a new one historically, has subtly captured the imagination of people who formerly took but a passing interest in it."

With those words, and well aware of the growing movement, we opened our introduction to the first edition of this book. But the fact that nearly a million copies have been purchased since its appearance eight years ago is testimony to a much wider audience and an enthusiasm even greater than we had anticipated.

In response to this warm reception, we have now revised our first edition with the goal of making it still more useful and challenging than its predecessor.

To keep you alert to the newest trends, we have included many examples of the very best contemporary designs by both professionals and amateurs; we have enlarged the section on flowers for the table to stir the creative talents of gracious hostesses; and we have expanded our section on prize-winning arrangements to encourage those who would like to participate in flower shows.

A salute to the garden clubs

For setting an example and showing beginners the way to the enriching enjoyment of flower arranging, we salute the women of garden clubs all over the world.

Through their sponsorship of flower shows and of classes in flower arranging, they have opened doors on a new world of artistic self-expression for countless numbers of people. The standards of excellence they have set, both for arranging and for judging, are universally respected and followed by flower arrangers everywhere.

We would also praise florists everywhere who have taken an interest in the amateur. They have generously offered expert advice and been the happy collaborators of arrangers in search of artistic ways to combine nature's gifts of the season. And they have made available an ever-widening choice of flowers and foliage throughout the year, happy to supply "a few of this" and "a little of that."

Today everyone can participate

The origins of the art of flower arranging go so far back into history that no one can be certain of its beginnings. Highly sophisticated designs with flowers can be found in the cultural records of ancient Egypt, China and Japan. But until quite recently this art was limited to the privileged few—either by patterns of culture or by the restrictions of economics.

Today, in contrast, anyone who has a small garden or access to a florist's shop can share in the pleasures of flower arranging without the need to expend large sums of money. In fact, the observing eye of a talented arranger will discover delightful materials for compositions in the commonest of weeds and grasses growing along the country roadsides.

And to combine with such readily available plant materials, rocks, shells and weathered wood are ours for the taking. A collection of such "found art" is twice rewarding—first in its gathering, and second in its use as an element of a satisfying design for an imaginative arrangement.

Whether you use flowers as a daily addition to your life, or as an occasional festive high light, this book will be both inspiring and helpful. Whether you are a beginner or an expert, there is much here that will be new and exciting to you. Whether you have but a handful of flowers or an armload, there are designs that will show you how to arrange them in fresh and imaginative ways. As you use this book, we know that you will grow steadily in your skill and appreciation of the rewarding art of flower arranging.

Chapter 1

Bring beauty into your home with flowers

When you enter a house and are greeted by the sight of fresh flowers and foliage attractively arranged, you know at once that you are in a home where beauty and hospitality are a valued part of gracious living.

The familiar phrase—"say it with flowers" —is truly meaningful because flowers do say special things for which it's often difficult, or impossible, to find the right words.

Everyone likes flowers on the table. They please the eye, help to whet the appetite, say that this meal will be a happy event, whether it is to be shared with guests or only by you and the members of your family.

Decorate with flowers

More and more people are coming to understand the great decorative assets of flowers throughout the home. The splash of vivid color in a bouquet can light up a neutral room scheme; white or pastel ones will freshen deeper hues. Gracefully arranged foliage can be used to soften severe architectural lines.

There is also a personal reward in selecting and arranging just the flowers that will do most to add to the beauty of a room. So many of the things in the world about us are necessarily mass-produced. But when you arrange flowers, you alone have selected and placed them in a design that's uniquely yours. To all who seek a creative outlet, flower arranging is surely a satisfying activity.

The art of flower arranging is not a difficult one to learn. Anyone who loves flowers and growing things—and will take the time to combine them with discernment—can acquire the necessary skills and techniques.

What makes the bouquet across the page so effective? It's partly that the cool, white contrast of the flowers sharpens the appeal of a rich green, purple and wood-toned background. It's also the way they're arranged, with an opulent air that's appropriate in a richly appointed room setting.

Pictures and ideas in this book will help you to work with flowers, to touch them with magic, to bring fresh beauty into your home.

Design with your setting in mind

An arrangement is most effective when it has been designed to suit a specific setting. The size, shape, and color of a flower composition should give evidence of its relationship to surroundings, be displayed in a container congenial to both flowers and decor.

For the same reason that it takes a tall woman to wear a large hat with grace, it requires a setting of generous dimensions to display a big flower arrangement suitably.

On a small table, a dainty arrangement is appealing and attention-getting because it satisfies our sense of proportion.

Color, discussed in detail a few pages farther on, is as important as scale to the success of an arrangement in a given room setting. But here there is a wide variety of valid choices one can make, because color contrast between flowers and setting is as attractive as a matching scheme.

A gold screen on the grand scale makes an impressive background for a boldly sweeping arrangement of magnolia and camellia foliage, with a vivid burst of red amaryllis bloom for a focal point. The sturdy bronze vase, the burl base, and the long, low table are all in correct proportion to the generous size of this arrangement which was designed by Mrs. Joseph Auner.

A Japanese tokonoma, or wall niche, here faithfully reproduced in a Western home, supplies an uncluttered background for a flower arrangement. The tokonoma is the center of a traditional home in Japan, and although we may not wish to copy it exactly, it teaches us a lesson in effective display: flowers grouped with a scroll painting and sculpture are mutually enhancing; and a proper setting—like a frame on a painting—increases our appreciation of any artistic creation.

French styling for a romantic arrangement of flowers in pastel shades of pink and lavender relates it to a feminine bedroom setting, with wallpaper in *fleur de lys* pattern. Delicate, curving lines of Scotch broom are used to give height and width to the design without making it too large for the small bedside table on which it is displayed. The elegance of a silver container suits both the flowers and their setting.

Use flowers as decorating accents

"Use flowers for accents" is the advice of decorators. And we all realize how much they can do for a room.

Flowers are lovely in themselves, but if we use them as decorating accents, we should first consider colors, style of furnishings, and size of room so we may design our arrangement in relation to the setting it will complement.

Color—discussed at greater length in a following section—is relatively easy to choose. Both matches and contrasts can be effective.

As important as color is style of arrangement. Modern and Oriental are "naturals" for contemporary rooms. A traditional arrangement looks best in traditional surroundings.

Warm colors of flowers inject a pleasant spicy note in a contemporary room whose furnishings run largely to neutral beiges and browns.

Amaryllis blooms, bronzy chrysanthemums and colorful croton foliage were combined in an arrangement designed by Mrs. Tommy Bright.

A symmetrical, pyramid shape was a good choice for an arrangement, placed where it can be seen from all sides.

Size of flower design is in scale with space for its display —neither too large nor too small. Simplicity of container suits the chaste air of contemporary room furnishings.

For a distinctive house,

an imaginative way

to put flowers into color

scheme of furnishings

A low chandelier that acts as flower container is as unusual as the room scheme it accents.

Fuschia velvet bows and candles set the dominant color note, with mixed flowers— all garden grown—of varied shades to harmonize with the decorating scheme.

A big, brass chain suspends the handwrought wooden chandelier of Mexican origin above a coffee table. Six glass epergnettes filled with saturated foam contain both flower arrangements and tapers.

This hanging arrangement was photographed at the home of the William Heusers.

Key flowers to their backgrounds

An accent color of this room, yellow, is repeated in an arrangement which reinforces a two-color room scheme.

Garden chrysanthemums take on new interest because their colors repeat those of the painting and pillows, contrast with blue furnishings.

White, bronze, and yellow flowers were cropped short, massed in a copper bowl.

Oriental arrangements are in tune with most rooms decorated in modern furnishings where the trend is to keep large surfaces plain, and show an interest in detail through accessories.

In keeping with the sophistication of the wall plaque, lamp base, and sculpture is a Moribana arrangement of red carnations and ti leaves by Minoru Saito, Flower Master.

Mass grouping of vibrant red tulips is right in both style and color for its casual and invitingly summery setting.

Informal wrought-iron furniture upholstered in cool blue-green flowered fabric calls for vivid color contrast and an unstudied bouquet.

The heavy, stoneware container is also well chosen for the setting, and is in the same garden mood as the furniture.

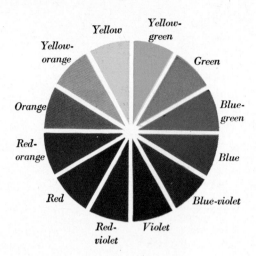

Color harmony in flower arranging

There's nothing hard to learn about color harmony applied to flowers. Nature's own color blends are so deft that it takes small skill to use them effectively.

Unlike pigments made by man, nature's colors are never "pure." Reds shade off to purple, and oranges to yellow in a single flower, so we shouldn't expect to match flower colors to decorating schemes as we can match paints.

Learning from the color wheel

Colors shown on the wheel above are the simplest or "purest" ones. They have been neither shaded nor tinted. If you add *white* to one of these basic hues, you'll get pastel *tints* such as many flowers display. Adding black produces *shades* or the grayed colors most used in decorating.

Even though flowers are not exact reproductions of hues on a color wheel, we can learn a great deal from it about combining and using flower colors to decorate.

The *monochromatic* color scheme is the simplest of color harmonies to recognize. It is merely a combination of the weaker and the stronger intensities of a single hue. Pink, rose, and red, used together, are a familiar example of monochromatic color harmony, often used in decorating.

Next, look for the *primary* colors. They are red, yellow, and blue. Various blends of the three account for all other hues on the wheel, whether it is the simple, 12-swatch wheel, or large color charts that include tints and shades of each hue.

Yellow and red we call "warm" colors; Blue is "cool." These are sometimes referred to as "advancing" and "retreating" colors. Notice that warm colors are concentrated on the left side of the wheel; cool on the right. Combine a warm and a cool color to achieve a pleasing effect.

Now pick out the opposite or *complementary* colors. They are the pairs which are exactly opposite each other on the wheel; violet is the complement of yellow; red of green. You get best effects from flower arrangements in complementary colors if the background is neutral.

Analogous or neighboring colors are the colors next to each other on the color wheel. Each contains much of its neighbor's hue, and because of this sharing of color they frequently make good partners.

Relate flowers to room colors

If you like to make decorative assets of your flower arrangements, you'll want to consider flower colors in relation to the color schemes of rooms in your home.

On the following pages we show you rooms decorated in monochromatic, complementary and analogous color schemes, with practical and easy-to-follow suggestions on ways to choose flower colors.

White is a combination of all colors, so it's always tasteful to use white flowers in a room— no matter what its colors.

But in the monochromatic color scheme room at right, white flowers placed as are the rosy chrysanthemums would be lost against the white curtains that serve as a background.

Green is always good. Take a lesson from nature and feel free to use green with any scheme.

Green in this room would be *complementary* to monochromatic red scheme of furnishings.

Violet hues will almost all be right in this rosy room because they are "neighbors" of red on the color wheel, with a bit of red in their composition.

Violet hues combined with the monochromatic reds of the room scheme would produce an *analogous* color combination. Imagine the attractiveness of a lilac or purple iris arrangement in place of the chrysanthemums on the white coffee table.

A monochromatic color scheme, in various tints and shades of red, is used to decorate this bedroom, with large amounts of white serving as a cool accent. Chrysanthemums that echo the room colors stand out against a background of white glass curtains. In another area of the room, against a rose or red background, white flowers would be good.

Fresh greens in a foliage arrangement are a possible alternate for this room, acting as a complementary color harmony in relation to the major furnishings. Also attractive would be flowers in a wide variety of violet hues, constituting an analogous color harmony.

In a room as formally furnished as is this one, with period chairs and a crystal chandelier, a more formal arrangement might act as a subtle reinforcement of the style of decor. The container should also be formal, perhaps of silver or crystal, to suit the character of the arrangement.

Color scheme flowers

Aim at a medley rather than a riot of color when you want
flowers to add to the beauty of your home. Unless yours is
a monochromatic scheme, flowers that repeat one or more of
the room colors will be most dramatic in enhancing decor.

Reds that are pure in hue or lean
toward orange will be best in
both rooms pictured here.

The purplish reds will clash
with oranges used in upholstery
fabric and accent pillows in the
blue-orange room at right.

Yellow is good in both rooms,
echoing colors that are already
present in furnishings.

Since yellow is a warm color, it
is always a welcome accent in
rooms that employ a large
amount of cool blue or green.

Analogous room scheme uses yellow and yellow-green against
an off-white background. Yellow and yellow-orange colors of
the daylily arrangement in a pewter vase are in good harmony
with the basic decorating colors of the room.

In a room whose color scheme is as restrained as this one,
there are few flower colors that would be unacceptable, but
against a neutral wall, the warm or advancing hues for flowers
will probably do most to enliven a rather quiet room.

Blue flowers wouldn't be wrong
in the room at right, but they
would only add more blue to a
to a predominantly blue room.

More effective in the room at
left, blue would be analogous to
the green that is part of a yellow-
green decorating scheme.

Exercise some restraint in the choice of flower colors for a complementary room scheme

Complementary color schemes as definite as the one in this room (blue-orange) are usually best served when flowers of the tints and shades already included in the room decor are used. In addition, green and white are always good.

The vivid orange of flowers in the arrangement pictured is a good choice since it repeats an accent color of the upholstery fabric and pillows, and brings inviting warmth to the predominant cool blues and greens of the room.

The principles of design

There are almost no "rules" that must be obeyed by flower arrangers. But there are some principles of good design you'll want to be aware of as aids to your own sense of taste and to your self-confidence.

Some happy few are born with so sure a feel for design that they put flowers together artistically without consciously following any principles of composition. But most of us grow in skill as we understand the fundamentals of design and use them to guide and test our arrangements. They are the same principles that all artists follow, not just flower arrangers.

On these pages we include sketches and simple diagrams to help you see the major elements that add up to good design.

Once you are aware of them, you'll feel freer to follow your own creative impulses as you shape designs with flowers.

Proportion

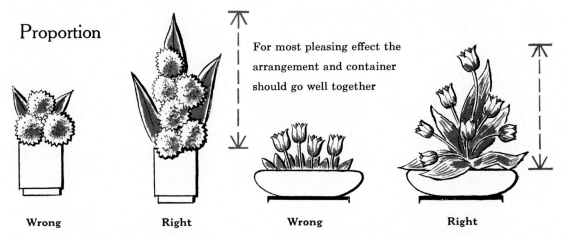

For most pleasing effect the arrangement and container should go well together

Wrong **Right** **Wrong** **Right**

Your flower arrangement is in good proportion when it seems the right size for its container. If you use a tall vase, a safe, general rule is to have height of flower materials which extend above rim equal to 1½ to 2 times the height of the vase.

Standard height rule for arrangements in low containers is that tallest stem equal 1½ to 2 times length or diameter of bowl. Experts in all styles ignore these "rules" as their skill and sense of proportion become well developed through practice.

Balance

We say flower arrangements look well-balanced when they give us a sense of stability—do not appear to be lopsided.

The two kinds of balance we may seek are: *symmetrical* (two halves are identical or nearly identical); and the *asymmetrical* (two halves are not actually equal but appear to our eyes to have equal weight or importance).

Symmetrical balance is relatively easy to secure. Asymmetrical balance requires greater practice, but can be more rewarding and challenging to our skill.

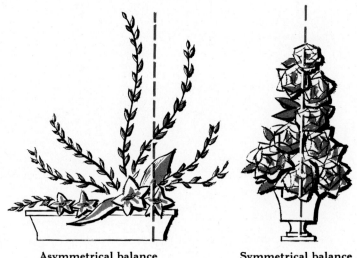

Asymmetrical balance **Symmetrical balance**

Seek contrasts of texture, color, form—or all three—to avoid monotony

Include *contrast* if you want more interesting arrangements. Combine rough with smooth, dark with light, round and spear.

Smooth texture   **Coarse texture**

Contrasting textures in an arrangement are easy to secure. Often you need only take advantage of nature's contrasts—soft velvety flower petals with shiny, glossy foliage; or coarse, ruffled petals with sleek leaves.

When the plant material you are using has no "built-in" contrast between flowers and foliage, use your imagination to make combinations that will offer good textural contrast.

Color contrast within a flower arrangement is gained by combining hues of greater and lesser *values*. Pale hues have less value than deep shades. Dark colors look best low in an arrangement, as they appear heavier to the eye. For help on choosing flowers to make the right color contrast within a room scheme, see the color section, beginning on page 14.

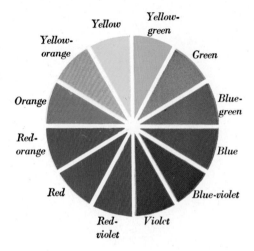

Round shape   **Spear shape**

Contrasting forms, like the rounded bloom and pointed leaf sketched at left, enhance each other when placed together. Deeply cut leaves are more interesting if combined with solid-looking flower heads. Often, the flower's own foliage is contrast enough. If not, search for others that give the wanted contrast.

Arrangements are harmonious when all elements are well blended

Harmony or unity is always your final goal in arranging flowers. It is a result of making a skillful selection of plant materials, containers, accessories, and setting so that they will appear to belong together.

If all these elements have been effectively blended, the outcome will be satisfying in design and will constitute a harmonious whole.

Basic shapes for arrangements

If you begin with a design in your mind, your flower arrangement is certain to be more successful than if you have no plan.

All arrangements except the Oriental and the Abstract tend to take on one or another of the shapes illustrated here. All, including these two, can be classified as either mass or line designs.

Next time you arrange flowers, select one of these shapes as your pattern. Of the several factors that must influence your decision about which shape to use, one is the kind of flowers and foliage you are working with. Some lend themselves to a design with height; others do not.

Another consideration is the placement of the arrangement—whether on the floor (tall), in the center of the dining room table (low and symmetrical), and so on.

Finally, the size and shape of your container must be taken into account. A tall vase requires height in the arrangement; a shallow bowl can display a low flower arrangement to good effect.

The triangular shape is adaptable

The triangle is a popular basic shape for symmetrical arrangements of traditional or modern style; it lends itself to many variations of height and width.

First step is to establish lines of height and width, usually with flowers or foliage of finer form or paler color. Next step is to establish a focal point of interest with larger or darker colored flowers at the center and just above the vase rim. Last is filling in with flowers of varied stem lengths, grouping colors rather than dotting them about at random.

The circular is satisfying

Nature must love the round or circular form since the majority of flowers do fall into that shape, from asters to zinnias.

Arranging them in circular designs adds a pleasing element of repetition that is satisfying to the viewer's eye.

Avoid monotony by using foliage that offers contrast to dominant round forms.

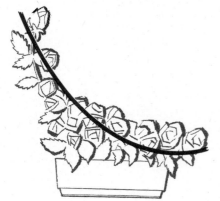

Crescent shape is an appealing line design

The crescent is asymmetrical, appeals to those of an esoteric taste, is rather formal in character. Its execution requires more skill and experience on the part of the arranger than do most of the mass-style arrangements.

Before attempting a crescent-shaped arrangement, make certain that stems of the plant materials you want to use are pliable enough to permit manipulation. Brittle stems, such as those of iris or gladiolus, will probably snap before you can bend them to the desired curve.

There's rhythm in the Hogarth curve

The English artist, William Hogarth, eighteenth century painter, once added a palette with an S-curve like the one below to his signature on a self-portrait, with the words "the line of beauty." From that incident we derive the name of this graceful style of line arrangement, a flower-show favorite.

The rhythmic line that distinguishes the Hogarth curve is easiest to achieve with vines or pliable branches of needled evergreen, using flowers to fill in at the center and just above and below the rim of a tall container.

Use a torch arrangement for height

The perpendicular line is often just what you need when you have limited display space. Some gladiolus and their own spear-shaped foliage are excellent for arrangements of this type, but many tall plant materials are adaptable.

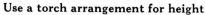

Convex curve shapes a centerpiece

The convex curve is a good line to follow when designing flowers for the center of the table. It does not need to be tall to be effective, and when it's kept low it won't interfere with across-the-table talk or view of the diners.

It is symmetrical, and thus attractive from every angle, an important consideration in an arrangement that is viewed from all sides.

Triangles face right or left, depending upon location

Flower arrangements conforming in shape to right-angle triangles appeal to modern arrangers because of attractive asymmetry.

Face the triangle to left or to right (as in the two sketches) according to the room location you have selected for the design.

If an arrangement is to be seen from two sides, remember to turn it around as you work, making certain that both views are equally attractive, finished.

Right-angle triangle arrangements are usually most effective in low rectangular containers.

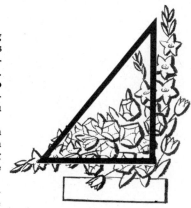

Three styles of flower arranging

Leading artists among flower arrangers—like artists in any medium—are likely to prefer one style to all others, finding it—after experimenting—most congenial to personal taste.

But to most of us, each style—Traditional, Oriental, and Modern—has its own charms. We enjoy experimenting with all three, depending upon our mood of the moment, kinds of leaf and bloom available to us, and the setting we have chosen for the arrangement.

Basic to Oriental style is emphasis upon *line* in every design. Traditional style is at an al-most opposite pole, achieving its most splendid effects with a *mass* of bloom.

Modern and its extension, Abstract, owe more to Oriental than to Traditional in concern with line. Both styles are unorthodox in use of materials, though Abstract pushes this furthest, sometimes making flowers and foliage entirely subordinate to container and accessories in order to sketch a scene, set a mood, or tell a story appropriate to the season.

We invite you to savor each style in its turn before you choose one as your favorite.

Modern and Abstract are, in flower arranging as in painting and sculpture, concerned with a personal interpretive expression.

In debt to the Oriental style for handling of line, these styles have no fixed rules or formulas for correct proportions. Their only test is the effect of an arrangement on a sensitive and knowing viewer's eye.

The arrangement at left illustrates the Modern and Abstract goal of using familiar materials in unusual ways. It employs driftwood and sculpture, as well as blooms of bird-of-paradise, so they are essential, not incidental to the design.

Oriental arrangements are more than aesthetic groupings of plant materials. They are, historically, symbolic presentations of an ideal harmony which exists between earthly and eternal life. They were, originally, displayed in temples.

In each arrangement there is a triangle. Its tallest line represents *heaven;* facing and looking to heaven is *man;* looking to both is *earth*.

There are many schools of Oriental arranging, each including styles that are formal or informal in nature. At left, the informal (Nageire) grouping demonstrates well the Japanese genius for revealing beauty in simplicity.

Traditional or period arrangements are typically full, symmetrical groupings of mixed flowers, such as the Victorian example pictured at right, displayed in a highly decorated china vase.

In mass arrangements, large bloom and deep hues are usually concentrated at the center; fine flowers or foliage and pale colors are used to outline the basic shape of the design.

The over-all form of a Traditional arrangement may be pyramidal, as it is here; or it may be round or oval, depending upon setting and plant materials.

It is in the European art tradition that this style has its roots, and arrangers who excel in it often find inspiration in antique flower calendars or in paintings by the old masters dating from the sixteenth and seventeenth centuries in Holland, France, and England.

Fan shape is typical of traditional flower arrangements of the Williamsburg period. Fine or feathery material placed at outer edges offers contrast to solid masses of bloom at the center.

Colonial flower arrangements were intended for placement on chests or sideboards, never on dining tables where arrangements of fruit were the only kind of decoration which was used.

Our colonial heritage

Flowers arranged in the styles loved by our colonial forefathers enliven the lovely old rooms of Colonial Williamsburg. And plants used in flower arrangements are the same varieties—native or imported—that grew in the gardens of eighteenth-century Virginia, as we know from flower prints and plant lists of that period.

Even containers for Williamsburg's arrangements are either originals of the period or careful reproductions of bowls and vases used by colonists.

Although fresh flowers are displayed in Colonial Williamsburg's exhibition buildings during most of the year, in fall and winter months visitors also enjoy the colorful compositions that feature dried blooms and foliage. For examples of these, see the later section on dry arrangements in period styles.

Gay marigolds, set off by their Delft brick container, are an unassuming garden annual made interesting by Miss Pennell's design which features buds and part-open as well as fully open blooms in a mass arrangement.

An authentic copy, the container reproduces a Bristol Delft jardiniere dating back to 1730.

Miss Edna Pennell, supervisor of flower arrangements for all of the exhibition buildings of restored Colonial Williamsburg, has held that position since 1956.

She is responsible for the daily creation of flower and fruit arrangements which complement each room's antique furnishings.

Mixed bouquets like this, reminding us of the fine old flower prints of eighteenth century—and earlier—European artists, were the favored style of arranging in colonial times.

It is, in fact, a study of these prints that guides today's Williamsburg arrangements and makes them true to designs of colonial times.

In the traditional style

The style of flower arranging we have come to call traditional is European in ancestry—mass grouping of mixed flowers such as have been immortalized in paintings of the Old Masters.

Always a popular way to arrange flowers in this country, our knowledge of this style has grown in recent years, thanks to the authentic arrangements displayed throughout the historic buildings of restored Colonial Williamsburg.

Authentic Eighteenth Century containers are used to hold all flowers gracing Colonial Williamsburg: fluted bowls, fingered posy holders, pitchers, jars, jugs, and tankards. Also shown are wire-mesh stem holders—standard equipment for traditional arrangements.

Opulence is a hallmark of the traditional style of flower arranging. It is exemplified at left by massed white dahlias, carnations, roses, and snapdragons in a silver-footed china bowl, the setting recalling a Chippendale era interest in Chinese taste, and a period when this style of arranging was universal.

Fan-shape of the generously-proportioned arrangement pictured below is typical of the Williamsburg style. Fine, feathery material—yew branches in this case—serves as background; tall flowers come next; big bloom as focal point; small, compact bloom to fill.

Oriental arrangements

Flowers arranged with artistry are constant decorations in Japanese homes. Displayed in an alcove called a "Tokonoma" which acts as a frame for the flowers, the arrangement is an indispensable part of a way of life.

Guests entering the home are made welcome, then brought to sit and admire the beauty of the flowers for a moment or two of tranquil silence before the ceremonial serving of tea.

Explore with us the symbolism behind the placing of each stem.

Tomoko Yamamato, Gekha-Soami School, first woman honored by the Emperor with the title Flower Master, created arrangements on these and next four pages.

Arrangements in the Nageire manner aim for simplicity and naturalness

First step is to establish three basic lines found in all Oriental arrangements: Heaven, the tallest line; Man, looking to Heaven; Earth, lowest and looking to both. Tallest stem is 1½ times over-all height. Secure the flower stems in a needle-point holder.

Second step is to place secondary flowers, called Mountain and Meadow. These are set into the triangle formed by the first three stems. All remaining flowers added to the arrangement must be "helpers," strengthening primary elements, not obscuring or conflicting with them.

Study these diagrams to learn basic principles of the Moribana style

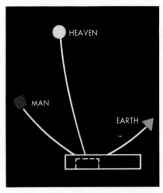 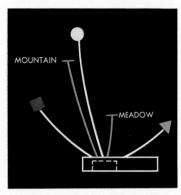 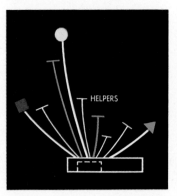 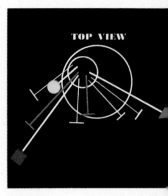

First diagram shows placement of three basic lines when Oriental arrangement is in Moribana style, in a low container. Heaven is 1½ to 2 times container width; Man ⅔ height of Heaven; Earth ⅓ the height of Heaven. In second diagram, Mountain is placed just behind Heaven, adding depth to the arrangement; Meadow is placed forward, as the lowest point in the composition. Third diagram shows how "helpers" are inserted to fill out design, but not conflict with primary lines. Fourth diagram, a top view, shows how Man and Earth lines project forward from Heaven line.

Arrangements in Nageire style are typical tea ceremony decorations

The Nageire style, according to fable, gets its name from an event of the Sixteenth Century, involving a famous general, Hideyoshi, and his favorite master of the tea ceremony, Rikyu, in the course of battle.

The day was hot and a temporary truce was declared to allow opposing generals time to rest and take tea. Rikyu looked about for some flowers —essential to a tea ceremony—and found iris growing nearby.

In lieu of a flower holder, Rikyu thrust his knife through a few flowers and an accompanying leaf, lightly tossed knife and flowers into a container of water, where it floated in an upright position.

Hideyoshi admired the promptness and ingenuity of Rikyu's action and exclaimed: "What a clever throw-in!" From that day on, such arrangements have been called Nageire, the Japanese word meaning a "throw-in."

Designs inspired by nature's lines

Every Japanese flower arrangement is, in a sense, a poem in praise of that life force which unites all things under the heavens. Originally, each arrangement had a religious symbolism, and this spiritual quality is present, even today, in compositions of the most gifted arrangers.

There is no desire to copy precisely an actual form such as one might see in a garden, but rather to pay tribute to an ideal form one sees only in one's mind.

In the beginning, Japanese arrangers considered it wrong to cut large quantities of living plant material with which to compose an arrangement. Instead, they cut the branches which would have to be pruned for the benefit of a tree or shrub; or they used flowers whose stems had been broken by the wind or other accident.

Although these restrictions are no longer honored, a basic admiration of economy continues to reveal itself in the artistry with which Japanese arrangers use a few stems to suggest many.

Through study and practice in the Oriental style of arranging, we Westerners can learn to look at growing things with a fresh eye. We can learn, too, how to use fewer flowers with larger effect, how to strip away details in order to reveal an essential form which is lovelier than man-made trimmings or decorations can be.

A single stem can be a composition in itself. A stalk of lilies, with bud, half-open, and full-blown bloom, symbolizes continuing growth in life.

Curving stalks of dictamnus are used for Heaven and Man positions. Iris leaves, gently manipulated, represent Earth. Largest purple iris, short and facing forward is Meadow; tall budded stem, Mountain.

Step one is to insert first three stems representing Heaven, Man and Earth lines. (Consult the Moribana chart at the top of page 29 for help in placing these major stems correctly.)

Use a large needle-point holder to secure heavy stems adequately. Pinch off undeveloped buds at the tip as they will probably not open.

A low bowl is always used for the Moribana style arrangement; it may be rectangular, round or oval.

Step two is to add the gladiolus stems to represent Mountain and Meadow. Mountain is slightly shorter than Heaven, and is placed just to its left and behind it. Its function is to give a sense of depth to the design.

Meadow is a short stalk, facing forward. It must be the lowest point in your entire arrangement.

These instructions are for an arrangement facing right. If the location calls for the opposite, reverse the position of each stem to get a composition that faces to the left.

Completed arrangement contains four more gladiolus stalks, making a total of nine. You could use 5, 7, 11, 13, 15, and so on, to get smaller or larger compositions. Only rule is that one should use odd rather than even numbers in order to achieve a pleasing, rhythmic total effect.

The Moribana style, latest to be developed by the Japanese, is suited to Western decorating tastes, combining naturalism of Nageire with the formality of classical styles.

Balance and harmony come first in Oriental arrangements

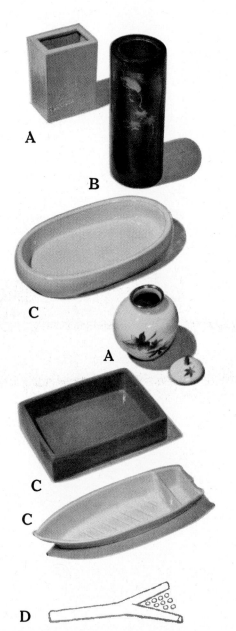

Primary lines, Heaven, Man, and Earth, should be placed first. Stems must be clamped tightly into holder (see sketch of kubari); no part of flower, stem or foliage may touch container. Position of three-legged usubata is also important: one leg must be center-front.

Second step is to add Mountain, Meadow. Mountain is cut a little shorter than Heaven and is placed slightly behind it, giving a sense of depth to the composition. Meadow line is low and at center, facing directly front. Additions must not obscure primary lines.

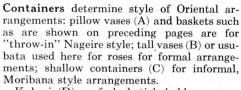

Containers determine style of Oriental arrangements: pillow vases (A) and baskets such as are shown on preceding pages are for "throw-in" Nageire style; tall vases (B) or usubata used here for roses for formal arrangements; shallow containers (C) for informal, Moribana style arrangements.

Kubari (D) or forked-stick holder secures stems in tall vase or usubata container. May be whittled by hand or purchased ready-made.

Oriental flower arrangements make symbolic interpretations of nature

Love of line is the motivating force that lies behind all styles of Oriental arranging. Unlike the Western attitude which puts flowers first and style of arranging second, the Oriental is primarily concerned with creating a balanced and harmonious composition. Even the humblest of growing things can convey beauty.

To attain an expert knowledge of classical Japanese flower arranging, one must be willing to devote years to study and practice. Few Americans have the opportunity —or the desire—to become true masters of this demanding art. But all of us can learn much from its basic principles.

One of the great delights of an acquaintance with the Oriental style of flower arranging is that it opens new vistas for our enjoyment. Suddenly we can see the essence of beauty in the lines of nature.

The formal or classical style, in which the roses pictured here have been arranged, is the one on which all the more informal styles have been based. Once a form of religious expression, and a part of the Buddhist worship ceremonies, it is used today without religious significance.

In this style, the goal is not so much to imitate nature as to make a symbolic interpretation of its underlying meaning.

In completed arrangement, helpers have been added, each reinforcing but not obstructing the primary Heaven, Earth, and Man lines shown in the step one picture at left. In an arrangement of mixed flowers, helpers should harmonize with colors of flower lines they reinforce.

Symbolism in Oriental arrangements

In the compositions of Flower Master Koshu Tsujii, exemplified by the three classic flower arrangements shown here, we have expressions of traditionalism and symbolism at their finest.

To the Japanese traditionalist, every plant has its season, and is seldom used except at the appropriate time of year. Plum, for example, calls to mind winter's end, and is special to February. Chrysanthemum, October's bloom, stands for immortality and has been the national flower for many centuries.

Flower arrangements of classic style reflect seasonal associations in other ways as well: spring is symbolized by burgeoning bloom, summer by luxuriant leaf, autumn by grasses and seed pods, winter by bare branches or evergreens that defy snow and frost to stay alive.

Symbolically, even the amount of water visible in a shallow container should rise or fall with the season: deeper in summer, shallower in winter.

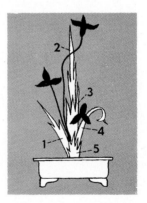

Three iris in a footed container are arranged in *chabana* style—suitable to place in a *tokonoma*, along with a wall hanging or *kakemono*. In front of them, the ceremonial tea service (*chanoyu*) is held.

Iris, of which many varieties are grown in Japan, are traditionally associated with Boy's Day festival. The upright growth pattern of the plant and its sword-shaped leaves may have had something to do with the association.

Follow the sequence of the numbered diagram just above in order to duplicate this precise, three-tier arrangement of iris.

*Arrangements which depict the beauties
special to the changing seasons*

Morning glory, held in high esteem by the Japanese, is symbolic of July.

It is often used in a hanging arrangement, as well as in a handled basket container such as this.

Vines are made to look as if they grew in their basket container, showing tendril, leaf, and bloom.

Top and side views of the arrangement are shown in the diagram at right.

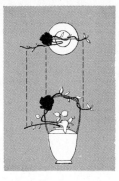

Budded branches of star magnolia have both strength and grace in their soaring lines which are complemented by two rosy tulips at the base of the composition, one faced forward, one up.

The rough texture of the black pillow vase—a classic shape long honored by Japanese arrangers—supplies a foil for the tracery of the branches and good contrast of color with paler flower tones.

Seasonal symbolism is evident in the use of flowering branches and bulbs and omission of foliage—characteristic of early springtime.

Symbolism in spring designs

These poetic compositions in honor of spring are the work of one of Japan's greatest flower masters, Koshu Tsujii. They were designed by him not long before his death in 1963, and illustrate the underlying symbolism which was characteristic of all his arrangements.

He was one of the last of the Kyoto group who had been trained from youth in classical *ikebana*, and who helped to develop the modern *moribana* style.

A number of Americans are familiar with his work, either from having been a student of his in Japan—he taught in the Daikakuji Flower Arrangement Academy of Daikakuji Temple—or from having observed his demonstrations when he made an extensive *ikebana* tour of the United States in 1960.

Symbolism in arrangements

Aside from the very evident beauty of arrangements such as these—easy for anyone to appreciate—we can also learn from them something of their symbolic meaning which we can apply to our own arrangements in honor of spring:

1. Select branches not fully leaved out to suggest the tender, new growth which characterizes this season.

2. Use flowers sparingly, remembering that spring's first few flowers are doubly precious for their very scarcity.

3. Observe closely and imitate growth patterns of nature in which voids are as important to design as filled spaces.

Soaring stems of pussy willow testify to the yearly miracle of spring. Seven stems were cut in varying lengths, then curved into gentle arcs. In column vases, traditional methods require using a forked stick only to secure stems. For those less skilled, it is possible to wire stems together first, fasten on snapdragons, then insert all in the forked stick.

Hawthorn branches are combined with tulips in a classical springtime arrangement. Two branches and three flowers form complementary triangles within the design.

Branches, symbolic of mountains or hills, give height to the arrangement; tulips, symbolizing the plains or a valley, are kept low.

The brass *usubata*, a traditional type of Japanese container, calls for the use of a *kubari* or a forked stick to secure stems. The Western arranger may, however, find he can attain greater stability by wiring branches together before inserting them in the forked stick.

Japanese tradition requires that, in an arrangement of this style, no flower or leaf should touch the rim of the *usubata*. Foliage must curve upward and out, not droop down.

Moribana arrangement proves the Japanese point that no growing material is too humble for inclusion in a flower composition if it is skillfully used. Here, hedge clippings, their tiny, bright green leaves just unfurling, are curved into a half-moon that frames the flowers.

In a central position, four daffodils of varying lengths are slanted so that one sees profile, side, and full views. They are accompanied by some of their own foliage.

Placed low and projecting at the right are three red carnations; small tufts of pine soften the transition.

A shallow container such as this one of rectangular shape is always used for arrangements in *moribana* style. Arrangement may face right or left, depending upon the setting in which it is to be displayed.

The modern style puts stress on line

Artist arrangers, like artists in the fields of music, painting, sculpture, and architecture, have broken with tradition in recent years to develop a contemporary style in which they feel at home, unbound by most rules of the past. The new school of arranging is called "Modern," or, still more recently, "Abstract."

Arrangements in the modern and abstract manner, original though they may be, reveal an indebtedness to the Oriental style in their stress on line and asymmetrical balance.

Also characteristic of modern and abstract arrangements is their minimal use of plant materials and frequent inclusion of an unorthodox container as an integral part of a composition—not just a holder of stems and water.

Mrs. Tommy Bright, designer of these arrangements, has a national reputation as a designer and teacher.

Coordination of flowers to colors of room furnishings increases the appeal of both. Yellow of snapdragons and chrysanthemums is an exact match for the yellow upholstery fabric of the nearby sofa. Dark, patent-leather gloss of croton leaves offers contrast of both color and texture.

Subtle similarity between the leaf pattern and the design on the container help account for the dramatic success of the composition. Just as important is the tapering shape and the height which relate this arrangement to its table-top placement.

One of the features that identify this arrangement as modern is its disregard of the rule that flower height equal 1½ to 2 times container height. Here, the flowers are almost 3 times as tall as the container, but are in pleasing proportion for this location.

Exotic accessories are a harmonious choice to serve as complement to the stark simplicity which characterizes many modern homes and their basic furnishings.

Their function is like that of intricate costume jewelry which fashion employs to sharpen the appeal of a basic dress.

Three anthurium spathes, with interesting tropical overtones, are in the spirit of the accessories which surround it. Arranged to follow a curving line, the design is reinforced with big philodendron leaves.

An Aztec motif on the pottery container makes its contribution to the total composition, but is not so bold that it distracts attention from the arrangement.

All-foliage arrangements that take advantage of natural contrasts make fresh-looking designs

Sansevieria leaves touched with white, lacy branches of lycopodium to soften contrast, are combined with branches of glossy cherry laurel placed low in an all-foliage arrangement for a modern interior.

Matching the black ceramic container are a tall vase and bottle showing the Scandinavian influence in their design. They are well placed on the buffet to balance the branch of cherry laurel flowing out from the foliage arrangement in an opposite direction.

Modern stresses line

Seven tulips in a striking crystal vase make a line arrangement which is deceptively simple in appearance. In fact, it takes skill to cut each tulip to the needed length, insert it in the desired position, and use just enough foliage to soften, not obscure, the basic design.

Nine daffodils, two still tightly budded, fashion a sophisticated line design with three croton leaves. The indebtedness of modern to Oriental styles is revealed both in the arrangement and in the base of stained bamboo on which rests woven-bamboo covered container.

Iris bud soars over a spring arrangement of daffodils and pussy willow to establish the height of a bold line design.

Two daffodil leaves are carefully manipulated, one to echo the angle of topmost bud, the other, in a downward curve, to balance the outward thrust of branches of pussy willow inserted at left.

The slender stemware container suits the attenuated lines of the arrangement.

Driftwood that resembles a piece of modern sculpture establishes the lines of a tulip and pussy willow design.

Needle point is nicely concealed by driftwood. In a big piece, it is possible to hollow out depression to accommodate a needle-point holder.

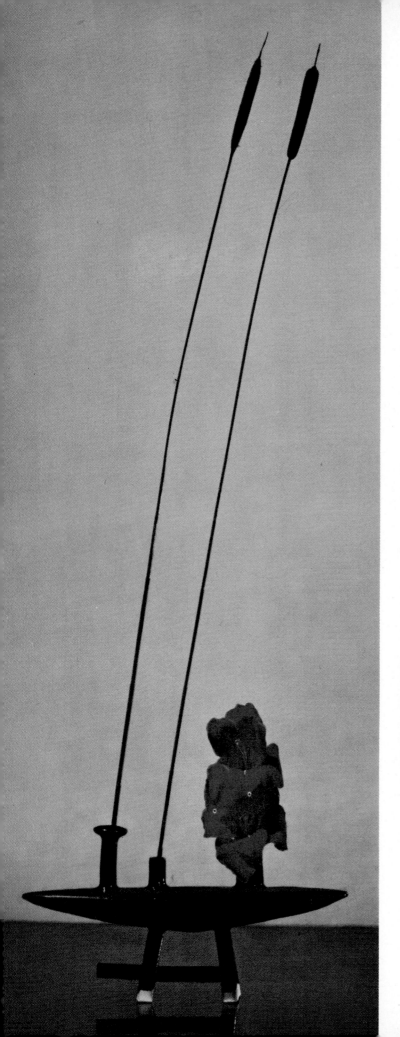

Abstract is news

To devotees of Japan's classical flower arranging traditions, the present interest on the part of leading Japanese and Western arrangers in the "abstract" style seems nothing short of heresy.

It is nonetheless true that there is currently world-wide enthusiasm for this school of arranging. And many who have earned the title of "master"—including Colonel Sparnon who designed the three arrangements pictured here—have turned to this style with great enthusiasm, believing that in it there is more freedom for personal expression.

Norman J. Sparnon, designer of modern Sogetsu arrangement at left—the exotic blacklacquered cattails leaning over a gladiolus stalk —is a "master" of both classical and modern schools of Japanese arranging.

This former Australian Army Colonel believes that, through this art form, East and West can better understand each other.

"Such stuff as dreams are made of," is the title of this fanciful abstract design, typical of Colonel Sparnon's dramatic style.

Its ingredients are dried bittersweet vine in loops and swirls above a black bottle vase with elongated neck, and one yellow rose.

The vine (wisteria might be substituted for bittersweet) was stripped of its foliage and twisted into the desired form while green, then allowed to dry. Painted black to match the vase, it is inserted in an upright position, with the yellow rose leaning slightly forward.

"The shape of things to come," features a highly unorthodox and primitive-looking container which was designed by one of Japan's foremost contemporary ceramic artists. Plant materials used are two pandanus leaves and five short stems of bronze chrysanthemums.

The boldness and daring of this design are characteristic of abstract. Although it seems bizarre and even grotesque to the uninitiated, this style is attracting many followers who are recognized experts in the traditional manner.

Fantasy and surprise characterize many abstract designs

There is an element of surprise in most abstract arrangements. It stems both from new uses of old materials and from use of unorthodox materials—as the lengths of plastic rod incorporated in one of the designs photographed here.

Nothing is barred, so far as abstract arrangers are concerned. Wires, bits of metal or plastic, painted or bleached stems and leaves—all these and more are acceptable if used imaginatively.

Veering away from tradition in another area, abstract arrangers are constantly seeking new kinds of containers. Some may be the work of leading contemporary potters; or they may be homemade "constructions" of daring design. Or arrangements may have no containers at all—in the conventional sense—materials being assembled instead on some kind of base.

Ikebana International

A consideration of abstract would be incomplete without mention of Ikebana International, a now worldwide association of arrangers, founded in Japan in 1956 by Mrs. Ellen Gordon Allen, one of whose arrangements is shown here.

Most of its members, including both Japanese and Occidentals, many of them well trained in classic Oriental schools, are today moving steadily away from the representative, toward the abstract. Their example has made itself felt everywhere as these arrangements testify.

Circular forms dominate an arrangement of *Allium gigantia*—its stems (bent while growing), its flower heads, the shape of the antique brass container. Saxifrage leaves give breadth at the base. This composition and the one at right are by Kathryn Holley Seibel.

Summer Abstract is the title of this geometrical design which opposes triangular and round forms arrestingly. Two stems of hemerocallis are framed by three spent stems and seedpods of iris, making a triangle that is balanced on a ball-shaped ceramic container.

Precise spiral of a spring which, with a metal
disk, forms the somewhat whimsical container,
is echoed by a loose spiral of dried kelp. Two
varieties of chrysanthemums—three of big
pompon type, the others of daisy-type—are
the living plant materials in an arrangement
designed by Mrs. Kathryn Holley Seibel.

The Square Root is the amusing title given
this arrangement by its designer, Ellen Gordon
Allen, founder of Ikebana International. A
modern Japanese container has two openings
to hold stems of cattails and anthurium. Surprise ingredient is a group of white feathers
obscuring vase openings from which stems rise.

World's Fair is the theme of this dry arrangement by Mrs. Merrill Cook. Teasel suggests
tall spheres; loops of matchstick bamboo the
highways and by-ways leading to the Fair;
crested red celosia for excitement. Treated
magnolia leaves at left lend visual balance.

Modern Christmas, arranged by Mrs. F. W.
Pickworth, establishes design with three rods
of clear plastic, uses seven white carnations
and tufts of pine to repeat the straight and
curving lines. Container is an up-ended glass
vase set onto a base of black painted wood.

Chapter 2

These aids make flower arranging easy

Like any art or craft, flower arranging requires good equipment. The essentials are relatively few and inexpensive.

All you really need—other than the flowers—are: three or four containers in the basic shapes; an assortment of needle-point holders and other stem-securing equipment; a sharp knife or flower shears; florists' tape and clay.

Shape, size and color of containers are of first importance. Until you become a collector of bowls and vases, shun those that are bright in color, strikingly patterned.

Neutral shades of off-white, green, gray, beige, and brown won't compete with flower hues. For the infrequent occasions when you *do* want something vivid, see if you can't make use of things you have about the house. An ash tray, a casserole dish, or a coffee mug may have hitherto unrecognized potentialities as a colorful and original flower container.

When you're selecting your basic group of flower containers, remember the importance of good proportion between size of bouquet and its container. Choose a variety which includes both large and small.

Needle points and other mechanical aids to secure stems are the foundation of an arrangement. Pictured opposite are examples of kinds on the market: needle points in many sizes and shapes; foam in rounds or bricks which can be saturated with water, keeping flowers fresh without a visible water supply; cage-type and hairpin-wire holders; crumpled chicken wire to stuff into tall vases.

A sharp knife is a possible substitute for flower shears, but it's more dangerous, less satisfactory for woody stems and branches. Or, you can treat yourself to a Japanese arranger's kit like the one pictured at the top of the page, including several cutting instruments designed for cutting and sawing woody stems.

Waterproof clay anchors needle points firmly when you're arranging tall, heavy stems that might topple. One valuable use—there are others—for a spool of florists' tape is to increase the size of stems too thin to be secured in a needle-point holder.

Eventually, you'll want a special place to keep your equipment. The storage cabinet pictured here is one you might like to copy.

Compartmentalized storage

Oriental arranging kit

Good mechanical aids can contribute much to the success of a flower arrangement.

Tips on cutting and preparing flowers

Flower	When to cut and how to treat
Anemone	½ to fully open. Scrape stems.
Aster	¾ to fully open. Scrape stems.
Azalea	Bud to fully open. Scrape and crush stems.
Bachelor-button	½ to fully open. Scrape stems.
Bleedingheart	4 or 5 florets open. Scrape stems.
Buddleia	¾ to fully open. Scrape stems or sear in flame.
Calendula	Fully open. Scrape stems.
Carnation	Fully open; snap or break from plant. Scrape stems.
Canna	½ to fully open. Scrape stems.
Chrysanthemum	Fully open. Break off and scrape stems or crush.
Clematis	¾ to fully open. Scrape stems.
Daffodil	As color shows in bud. Cut foliage sparingly or bulb will not mature. Scrape stems.
Dahlia	Fully open. Sear stems in flame.
Daisy	½ to fully open. Scrape stems or sear in flame.
Daylily	¾ to fully open. Flowers last just one day.
Delphinium	¾ to fully open. Scrape stems; snap off top buds.
Geranium	Fully open. Scrape stems.
Gerbera	¾ to fully open. Sear stems in flame.
Gladiolus	As second floret opens. Scrape stems; snap off top buds.
Heliotrope	¾ to fully open. Sear stems in flame.
Hollyhock	¾ to fully open. Float florets or scrape stems.
Hydrangea	Fully open. Sear stems in flame.
Iris	As first bud opens. Do not cut foliage; scrape stems.
Larkspur	¾ to fully open. Scrape stems; snap off top buds.
Lilac	½ to fully open. Scrape and crush stems; float wilted branches in 110-degree water for an hour.
Lily	As first bud opens. Cut no more than ⅓ of stem or bulb will not mature. Scrape stems.
Marigold	Fully open. Scrape stems.
Mignonette	¾ to fully open. Sear stems in flame.
Morning-glory	In evening when closed. Wrap each bud in soft paper, sear vine stem; let stand in deep water overnight.
Narcissus	As color shows. Cut foliage sparingly; scrape stems.
Nasturtium	½ to fully open. Use with its own foliage.
Peony	Bud in color to fully open. Scrape or split stems.
Poinsettia	Full color. Sear stems and points from which leaves have been removed.
Poppy	Night before opening. Sear stems; drop of wax in heart of flower keeps it open.
Rose	As second petal unfurls. Cut stem just above a five-petal leaf or plant will stop blooming. Scrape stems.
Snapdragon	¾ to fully open. Scrape stems; snap off top buds.
Stock	¾ to fully open. Scrape stems; snap off top buds.
Sweetpea	¾ to fully open. Snap stem from vine.
Tulip	Bud to ½ open. Cut foliage sparingly; scrape stems. Wrap flowers in paper; stand in deep water overnight.
Violet	½ to fully open. "Harden" by soaking in water for half-hour then wrap and refrigerate.
Waterlily	Tight bud. Sear stems in boiling water; drop of wax in heart of flower keeps it open.
Zinnia	Fully open. Sear stems in flame.

Professional tips that will improve arrangements

Best way to carry cut flowers from the garden is in heads-down position. Heavy-headed flowers won't snap off.

Lay flowers flat, wrap in newspaper. Plunge bunch into tepid water for 3 to 5 hours or overnight to condition.

To revive wilting flowers, snip off a half-inch of stem under water and plunge in deep container of water.

Shape leaf to resemble its original proportions when you must trim away a brown spot along its margins.

Never place a finished arrangement where it will be exposed to draft of a fan, window, or to full sunlight.

To repair the bent stem of a heavy-headed bloom, insert toothpick to run through center and into stem.

Many flower and foliage stems are quite pliable and can be curved by placing thumbs together and bending.

Keeping or reviving woody stems depends on prompt pounding of bottom two inches before plunging in water.

To insure lavish intake of water by woody stems, pare off bark from bottom two inches and crosscut stems.

There are tricks to all trades—flower arranging included—that help make results more professional-looking. Here are some used regularly by florists and by experienced arrangers. They'll serve you in good stead also. They'll make cut flowers stay fresh longer, speed your job of assembling an arrangement, guarantee a handsomer finished design.

Study these eighteen tips for better technique. Whenever you're making a flower arrangement, put them into practice. You'll find that they work!

To reduce underwater decay, strip the stems of all foliage and thorns which will fall below the water line.

Bloom of some flowering shrubs has a tendency to wilt. To reduce problem, clip off small shoots at top.

Dahlias, poppies and other flowers with hollow stems should have stem ends seared to prevent sap escaping.

Roses and tulips open rapidly in a warm room. Use twist of tape to keep blooms from opening while arranging.

You can prolong the freshness of an arrangement by spraying with a syringe of tepid water morning, night.

Candle wax dropped at base of flower head keeps bottom petals from falling off flowers like chrysanthemums.

To secure stems of flower arrangements using large branches, stuff container with crumpled chicken wire.

Insert stick to strengthen weak, hollow stem of such flowers as gladiolus; be sure stem bottom reaches water.

Y-shaped forked branch may be cut to fit neck of tall vase or narrow container and hold flowers upright.

It's satisfying to own the right containers

Next to the flowers themselves, the right container is the most important part of any arrangement. As a beginner, you'll need only a few—such as the four pictured at the upper right-hand corner of the facing page. But as you grow in skill, you'll inevitably want to expand your collection of bowls, vases, and other containers. Here's an array to hint at the exciting variety which awaits you.

Black pottery vases, mostly Japanese in origin, are dramatic flower containers.

Pewter-washed copper containers, heavily embossed or simple in decoration, fit in comfortably with period or modern furnishings.

Italian pottery vases, contemporary in style, are often strikingly patterned. This limits their versatility, but when used with foliage-only arrangements, or dried materials whose colors are harmonious, nothing can be more gratifyingly appropriate.

Heirloom pieces, or modern reproductions of them, are ideal containers for flowers designed in period styles. Eighteenth Century and Victorian tastes approved of floral designs on flower containers, and this style is gaining in popularity today as Victorian furnishings have again come into fashion.

For an example of one way to use the cherub-borne porcelain bowl, see the mixed arrangement featuring roses shown on page 83.

Glass and crystal containers are demanding when used with long-stemmed arrangements where stem lines are visible. But, well used, their sparkle compensates for the extra pains.

Basic shapes of these four containers make them an excellent first collection for a beginning arranger. A good average size would be from 9 to 12 inches in height or width.

The classic beauty of silver will remain forever in fashion. Use it with both modern and traditional arrangements.

Exercise your imagination to discover new containers in household objects you already own

Classic Japanese containers are: bronze usubata; gilded column vase; low, square bowl.

Household objects like ash trays, pitchers, mugs, and goblets, double as flower holders.

Beauty in simplicity is a quality an artist looks for. So does the artist-arranger. A common bean pot, stone jug, or an individual casserole might be the handsomest possible container for informal bouquets of garden flowers or autumn grasses.

Nature's sculpture is yours for nothing more than the trouble of searching it out in the course of travels. Depending on where you go, you'll find: a manzanita branch, a water-smoothed fragment of driftwood, a twisted piece of sagebrush. Each will be unique, yours to use creatively.

Sea shells can function as containers as well as accompaniments to flowers, as Mrs. Kathryn Holley Seibel shows us in an imaginative design of hemerocallis.

Large rock simulating nearby mountains, white chrysanthemums at its base, constitutes the foreground in a miniature landscape by Tomoko Yamamoto. A sheared and precisely bent branch of juniper evokes a distant Mount Fujiyama.

Nature's art is yours to use

The ability to recognize beauty in unexpected places is characteristic of the most gifted arrangers. To the uninitiated, a rock is a rock, a shell a shell. But to the artist arranger, each is a treasure that can enhance the beauty of flowers and foliage with which it is combined.

A stroll in the woods or along the edge of the sea becomes a real adventure, once you've learned to look for curiously shaped bits of wood, shells, and water-smoothed rocks and pebbles—all things you might once have ignored.

Miniature scenes from nature such as the Japanese excel in are eminently suited to "found art." Or, as the arrangements pictured suggest, a shell can be a container; rocks and weathered wood can be a part of a landscape; or they can be attractive masks for mechanics of an arrangement, lend a finished look to your compositions.

Collecting rocks pays when flower arranging is your hobby. Of course you use rocks and pebbles to disguise a needle point. But don't forget that they can be extremely effective as the dominant feature in an arrangement which seeks to call up the image of some remembered landscape.

Autumn in Verlot by Mrs. Marguerite Bozarth is a happy reminder of a camping trip. The dry ferns, a weathered branch, piece of driftwood recall haunting sounds of wind and water flowing down to Puget Sound.

Infinite variety and appeal of shells is too seldom appreciated by flower arrangers. Employ them as a rich source of intricate patterns, shapes, and colors. Use them in your arrangements of plants that normally grow near the water.

Ceramic figures of good design (most of these are imports) are a worthwhile investment. Take a tip from the Japanese and never place a figure in water unless it represents an animal that normally lives in or under the water.

Brave bulls and a torch of spring flowers (ranunculus and narcissus) make a dramatic end-of-the-table decoration for a gala Mexican or Spanish dinner party.

Cup-type needle-point holder has been hidden from view by flowers and foliage. Wisps of Scotch broom give height.

Wild parsnip, with flower heads gone to seed, is the only plant material you need for this Nageire-style arrangement, in a Japanese basket container of bamboo with a tin liner.

Small, beautifully carved wood toad, a Japanese import, is an appropriately woodsy companion for an informal arrangement. He appears to be admiring a design that uses weeds so stylishly.

This seldom-used but arresting plant is yours for the gathering along early summer roadsides. Or, you might use Queen Anne's lace or dill from your own vegetable garden in the same manner.

When to use figures with flowers

The best rule for using figures with flowers is to include them only if they are both artistic and appropriate to help tell the story or advance the theme of the arrangement you wish to create.

If they're just an afterthought, or if they have no intrinsic beauty of their own, they should be omitted as distractions rather than additions to the beauty of the flowers that are of primary interest.

When figures or sculpture are to accompany any arrangement, make certain they are in correct scale—neither too small nor too large to balance the size of plant materials and container you use.

Spring scene in miniature is composed of three yellow early crocus blooms and a little grasslike foliage, a cluster of fungus such as you find on old logs, bits of moss, a fledgling ceramic bird, and an inquisitive green grasshopper.

A round chartreuse straw place mat acts as a frame for the scene.

Madonna of frosted crystal, surrounded by Easter lilies and yellow tulips sets a religious theme with taste and restraint.

The madonna figure was secured in the center of a needle-point holder with florists' clay. Then the tulips, with some of their own foliage, were inserted as background to madonna.

Short-stemmed Easter lilies, each cut to a different length, face forward and up, with one bloom projecting outward from the rim of the clear glass bowl container.

At Christmastime, pine branches with roses in a similar arrangement would make good seasonal substitutes for the tulips and Easter lilies.

Bases for flower arrangements

To give a finished look to a flower arrangement, many arrangers use bases. They may be of teak, straw, bamboo, polished or painted wood of all kinds. You may even want to use a mirror.

In addition to a sense of completeness which a base or mat can provide, it may do two other things: extend the dimensions of an arrangement so it more adequately fills a large area; or improve the apparent balance of a tall flower composition in a slender vase, keep it from looking precarious.

Ready-made burls come in many sizes and finishes. But if you're deft at simple carpentry, you can make your own by following the pictures and instructions on the facing page.

When selecting a base, keep in mind the style of the arrangement—formal or informal—and choose one to match.

Burl bases themselves are not limited to use with strictly informal arrangements. They are in excellent taste as finishes for semiformal arrangements in oriental or modern style.

End-of-summer arrangement by Mrs. Merrill Cook combines forsythia foliage, gloriosa daisies, colorful Indian corn, and a ceramic pheasant. Flowers and foliage are inserted in a cupholder type of needle point that supplies necessary water but is not visible. The rather roughly finished burl base is in harmony with the informal style of the autumnal arrangement.

To start, you need a tree stump that's been weathered by sun, wind, and rain for at least several months. Osage orange—like this piece —is a good choice because of hard, attractive grain. Or use oak, hard maple, cherry, or other fruit woods. With a handsaw, remove an oblique slice about a half-inch thick.

Next step: sand burl to a perfectly smooth surface. Wrap sandpaper around a block of wood for easy handling. Use it to sand both sides until roughness is gone. If wood color is too light to suit you, stain to desired shade. Next, brush with clear varnish. Let dry. Sand again before applying more coats of varnish.

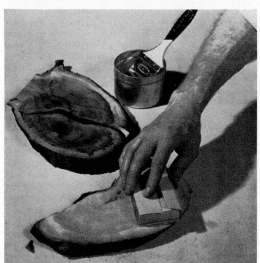

Finished burls in assorted sizes have a number of uses in addition to serving as bases for your flower arrangements. They add to the effectiveness of a favorite piece of sculpture, or may be used as stands to protect table tops. An advantage of making your own burl bases is that you can have right size for each container. Be sure the base you use is comfortably larger than the container it accompanies.

Ready-made bases for your flower arrangements come in a very wide range of colors and styles, as the sample below suggests.

Each of the base styles pictured also comes in a variety of sizes—small, medium, and large —to harmonize with the size of the container which it is to accompany.

In photographs throughout this book you will see many styles of bases used. Study them to see which types you might like to own before you buy or make your own collection.

What to do with a dozen roses

Next time you buy—or are given—a dozen of one kind of flower, play the game of dividing the florists' dozen into two or three arrangements. It's more fun than using all of them in one bouquet, and it pays big dividends of fresh beauty for several settings—not just one.

New tricks with twelve

First, decide on the places where you want to put the groups of flowers. Would you like them in the center of the dining room table, on the buffet, on a hall, occasional or coffee table? Perhaps a desk needs brightening with flowers.

Next, choose containers to suit the locations you've chosen to decorate with flowers. Use tall vases or low bowls, depending upon the amount of height that you want in the particular setting.

Now divide the bunch into the groupings you've decided on. If one of the arrangements is to consist of a single flower —as in the one across the page—choose the biggest, most perfect bloom for it. Attention will focus on it, just because it's alone, more sharply than on individual blooms in an arrangement of several.

Play up the foliage, too

Florists ordinarily include extra foliage such as salal, huckleberry, or other greens with a bunch. Often the blooms will have their own luxurious foliage, like the leaves on these roses. Let foliage help you fill in and vary your designs.

One perfect rose has universal appeal. Here's a way to use it so it's an "arrangement" in itself.

This design uses salal (commonly called lemon leaves and carried all year around by most florists) foliage to make a green frame for one glowing rose.

If your roses—or other flowers—have good, fresh foliage, you can use it equally as effectively to expand dimensions and give an important look to one bloom in similar fashion. If not, use clippings of your shrubs or even house plants as accompaniment to single flower designs.

This container, an appealing ceramic imitation of a sea shell, contributes its share to the dramatic appearance of the flower in both shape and sharp color contrast of ivory with red and green of roses and foliage.

Dining table centerpiece uses nine more roses from our florist's dozen in a symmetrical design, kept low so it won't interfere with across-the-table conversation. Rose stems are held in place by a piece of hardware cloth that covers the top of the crystal container. It's out of sight, thanks to careful placement of the foliage.

Roses for this arrangement were cut to varying stem lengths, faced in slightly different directions so that each diner would have an equally attractive view. To extend the length of the arrangement, two stems were placed horizontally. Notice that the two largest blooms were placed lowest and at center, one facing you, the other in corresponding opposite position on the side of the container that is hidden from view in this photograph.

Crystal goblet makes an imaginative substitute for a conventional vase to hold a simply styled arrangement using two blooms. A bud vase would, however, be an equally suitable container for a tall two-flower arrangement designed for placement on an end table.

The two roses, with their own foliage, were cut to different lengths and inserted in a tiny needle-point holder which was first secured in the bottom of the goblet with florists' clay. (If you have a bud in your bunch, use it for the taller of the two stems.) Additional foliage was inserted to give attractive fullness to the design.

After roses and foliage were placed, some clear-glass marbles were dropped into the goblet to add further interest and to obscure stem lines and needle point.

All three of the rose arrangements pictured on these pages were designed by Mrs. Cummins Rawson.

Simplicity has universal appeal

Most of us would like nothing better than to have flowers always about the house. We know they add freshness and beauty in a way that nothing else can do so well.

But we often forego that pleasure because we haven't fully realized the virtues of simplicity, and the attractive results we might obtain with just a few flowers.

Simplicity *does* have real charm, and it is basic to the design of all the arrangements pictured on these two pages. Let them convince you never to do without flowers when it's so easy—and inexpensive—to have them with you.

Two red roses in a white ceramic bud vase are the sole ingredients of this appealing arrangement. Curving line of stem, glossiness of foliage, freshness of bloom are enough to make you want to look and look again.

Siberian iris foliage is featured in this arrangement, with a few seed pods and a stem of German iris to add color and variety. Arrange leaves in your hand, secure with a rubber band before inserting them on the needle holder.

Short stems of pink and red geraniums with their own foliage are placed so that a few blooms are high, the rest low, in a bowl that is a good match for one of the flower colors.

Remember this arrangement when, at end of summer, geraniums in border or window box are blooming bravely, but will soon be taken by frost.

Two carnations in a shade to match the upholstery of the nearby armchair take on importance because of the way they have been arranged.

Glossy camellia foliage supplies a frame for the flowers, and a footed container of milk glass lends necessary height.

Scale, color, and traditional styling that suit the setting are all factors in the success of this small arrangement.

Red bowl gives impact to a casual group of single white peonies, both bud and full-blown, accompanied by their own deeply-cut foliage.

The small needle-point holder on which the standing stems are secured is concealed by foliage and floating bloom.

Other garden flowers which might be used in a similar arrangement include: tuberous begonias, early double tulips, camellias, and water lilies.

A single spike of gladiolus with ruff of philodendron leaves is displayed in an Eighteenth Century porcelain basket which contains a low cup for water and a needle-point holder.

All of the undeveloped buds were first removed from the end to get flower color right up to the tip of the gladiolus spike.

Arrange these in just a few minutes

Caladium leaves—use uneven numbers for rhythmical effect—are all you need for this satisfying composition to decorate a dining-room table.

What makes this arrangement special is simplicity of effect, gained by careful placement that lets each leaf stand alone, yet be a part of the satisfying total composition.

White pebbles hide from view the needle-point that holds the stems in place.

One canna stalk (at right) with its own foliage supplies quick, effective color. If you've never thought of using this common garden plant for a flower arrangement, here's evidence you've been missing a good bet.

Cut the canna spike to 1½ or 2 times the diameter of a shallow container. Center the stem on a small needle-point holder.

Arrange 6 leaves to encircle the blooming stalk as shown in the picture. Place two of the larger leaves low, giving breadth at the base of your single-flower composition.

Use small white pebbles to disguise needle-point holder and lend finish to your design.

Hibiscus blooms (at left) are pretty in a pitcher or floating in a saucer. If you have beautiful flowering shrubs in your garden, do clip a few of the blooms and branches—judiciously, of course, so as not to injure plants—to put on display inside your house.

There needn't be anything fussy about your arrangement. Select an informal type of container to contrast in color with the plant material. Prune as necessary to emphasize the free-flowing, natural growth lines.

In summer, a flower floating in water makes a cool freshener for almost any spot in a house.

Chapter **3**

Enjoy each of the seasons in its turn

A newly creative way of looking at every growing thing is one of the life-enriching pleasures that an interest in flower arranging brings with it, helping us recognize beauty we once ignored.

All seasons shall be sweet to thee
Whether the summer clothe the general earth
With greenness, or the redbreast sit and sing
Betwixt the tufts of snow on the bare
    branches
Of mossy apple-tree.

S. T. Coleridge

The magic rebirth of nature which takes place each spring gains added meaning once we learn to look for its special symbols: bloom that appears before leaf, shy green of newly emerging foliage, rich colors of rain-moistened earth. Most of us, until we begin to use them in flower arrangements, have never fully appreciated subtle differences in foliage greens that make spring so unlike the summer to follow. Then every leaf and blade will finally seem to have been dyed to a uniform shade.

Summer overwhelms the flower arranger with her riches. Leaf and bloom are so abundant that, were it not for our skill as designers, we might be satisfied with simple riots of color. But, again, from having learned to observe nature closely, we will see greater beauty we can bring to arrangements through contrasts of texture and form—round shapes combined with spears, velvety surfaces set off by juxtaposition with glossy ones.

Autumn's arrival is more eagerly anticipated when we learn to recognize beauty in sere grasses and dry seed heads of the season as well as in the tapestry of colored foliage that dominates the end-of-summer landscape.

Finally, when winter comes, the true test of our ingenuity and resourcefulness arrives with it. Gnarled wood, sprigs and branches of evergreen, perhaps a few fresh flowers from the greenhouse—these and our newly awakened imagination are all it will take to succeed. From these we can produce designs that bespeak the season, yet introduce touches of welcome green into our winter-bound homes.

Spring's rebirth

Winter's greens

Summer's riches

Autumn's harvest

Designs for a few flowers

Let your spring designs be symbolic of the beginning of a new growing cycle. Barren winter has ended, and the burgeoning season—awaited so long—has at last begun. We appreciate each new bud and leaf.

In the same way, spring arrangements for our homes can make a virtue of scarcity. A few flowers at this time of year will give as much pleasure as armloads can later on, when summer bloom is bountiful.

A few tulips of mixed varieties plus long, flowering branches are the ingredients for an impressive arrangement. This is the time of year to seek the sweeping lines that make such a dramatic effect in designs such as this.

Let one tall branch soar skyward and a second trail gracefully over the edge of a table or chest. Add cut flowers as the focal point. You won't need many!

It takes just five stems for this well-proportioned arrangement

First, place tallest stem, 2 times the length of 7-inch bowl. Cut second stem 10 inches long; slant left. Trim third stem to 9 inches. Place low; slant right.

Next, cut a daffodil 12 inches long and put it back and left of tallest bloom. Place 8-inch stem directly in front of tallest one; include foliage for contrast.

Speak of spring with a bright grouping of white narcissus and yellow daffodils

In early spring you may discover you have a few blooms from each of several types of narcissus. By all means cut them—they'll make a lovely arrangement.

Choose a long, shallow container; anchor a needle-point holder in it with florists' clay. Place it off-center. Now you're ready to begin building a design.

Select the tallest stem with the smallest flower and cut it to 1½ to 2 times the length of the bowl. Cut other stems to varying lengths, remembering that taller ones should have smaller blooms, shorter ones the larger flowers. In the arrangement shown, yellow, double blooms were the obvious choice for the focal point; three tulips would make a good substitute. Cut foliage sparingly, but use some for contrast.

Tulips and flowering plum are as beguiling as a pink cloud in this springtime arrangement. Cut 7 branches and 7 blooms for a low container. The tallest of your branches should measure twice the length of the bowl, its tip slanted over the center.

Capture springtime with flowering branches and bulbs

One day, toward winter's end, when you feel you can't wait longer for spring to arrive, go cut branches of flowering shrubs or trees to bring indoors.

Be judicious. You don't want to mutilate a parent plant, and you won't if you take branches that should be pruned later. You'll have best luck if you start the forcing process about a month before the particular tree or shrub would leaf out normally. Plunge branches in warm water and give them lots of light as they open.

Still-bare branches of flowering crab have a delicate tracery which needs only a handful of daffodils to bring spring indoors on the dreariest of late winter days.

You'll have the pleasure, as you enjoy the arrangement, of watching buds swell, tiny green leaves emerge.

Green leaves have begun to appear by the time daffodils fade. Now we might replace them with some yellow daisies as a new focal point for our springtime arrangement.

The leafing-out process will take about a week in the indoor warmth.

Flowers commence opening on the branches of crab-apple during the third and fourth weeks indoors.

When a change of flowers is in order, an assortment of bloom such as tulips, daffodils, and snapdragons would make a charming variation.

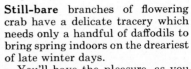

Lilacs and tulips combined with Oriental artistry remind us of a bed of tulips abloom beneath a luxuriant lilac bush, its branches heavy with the fragrant lavender plumes of spring.

The Earth line is represented by one short branch of deeper purple lilac. Tulips in harmonious rose and purple shades take the Meadow position in a subtle Moribana composition.

Perfume the air with lilac plumes

To delight our senses of sight and smell, few springtime flowers can excel the lilac. Deep purple of still-closed bud tip shades off delicately to paler tones at the base of each fresh flower head. Every plume is a sweet-scented composition, complete and satisfying in itself.

White and blue lilacs do not have self-contained color variations like those of their more traditional purple cousins, but they have greater sophistication—a quality which endears them to many. It is easy to imagine a properly placed bouquet of white lilacs bringing a whole room to life.

Should you prefer to use lilacs alone, instead of with tulips as in our mixed arrangement, the bloom heads with their own heart-shaped foliage are quite sufficient.

Try an informal grouping in a silver or pewter water pitcher to see how the sheen of metal enhances the soft, feathery look of the flowers through contrast.

Important to success—whether you use lilacs alone or in combination with the bright, spring-flowering bulbs that come to bloom at the same time—is careful pruning.

It's a common fault of beginners to drown lilac bloom in a great sea of green leaves. To avoid this, study each branch to discover its natural curves of beauty. Then prune away the growth that distracts from those lines you wish to emphasize.

Another problem for beginners is preventing lilac branches from wilting. Follow the directions below to keep them fresh.

Lilacs won't wilt in arrangements
if you prepare them properly

Remove from the base of the branch all foliage you will not need in your arrangement. Then split the end of the branch by pounding it with a hammer; or make cross cuts with sharp flower shears for a distance of an inch or two before placing in water.

The purpose of crushing the bottom of the branch and removing the bark is to permit quick and ample absorption of water. A small cut across the stem end will not expose sufficient surface to water.

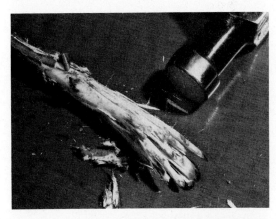

Submerge pounded stem in denatured alcohol for *only* 3 to 5 minutes before placing in fresh water as an added guarantee that branches will stay fresh, not wilt in arrangements.

This treatment is effective for all branches with woody stems.

Wide-apart bloom heads could give a spindly look to an arrangement.

You can correct this by using florist's tape that matches the color of bark to pull the two flower heads closer together. Place so tape won't show.

Revel in color with garden iris

The regal bearded iris comes to us in so eye-delighting a pallette of colors that one of its hues is sure to harmonize with your color scheme. Their range runs from an almost snowy-white to cream and yellow, pink, sky blue, a nearly-crimson hybrid and all of the lavenders and purples.

Bearded iris—like most of the big singles used in the arrangements pictured here—don't travel well. Bring them straight in from the garden and arrange them immediately.

If you have no garden iris, Dutch iris which your florist carries for a good portion of each year are considerably less fragile and can be used similarly, although their range of colors is more limited—mostly blue, yellow, and white.

To the Japanese, there is much symbolism surrounding the arrangement of iris. In classical styles, the season is interpreted by the position of flowers: if bloom rises above foliage, it is spring; if foliage is taller than bloom, this is an indication that summer is on its way.

Tallest stalk should measure 1½ times the length of low bowl; second iris ⅔ height of tallest; third stem ½ height of the first.

Add four more stalks of yellow iris, each stem a different length. Insert two stems to right and two to left of the central line.

Deep purple of several varieties of iris combine strikingly with yellow and white. Small star-shaped Siberian iris form a triangular frame for bearded iris.

Two feathery spikes of gasplant offer pleasing contrast to the rounded forms of iris and of white peonies, inserted at the lower left. Peony foliage and a large rock help to obscure the "mechanics."

No two flowers are placed at exactly the same level or angle, and lines of some of the stems flow out of the container, avoiding a "flat" look and giving an appearance of depth to the arrangement.

In general, iris are most appealing in arrangements that focus attention on their graceful lines rather than on mass effect of bloom. They combine harmoniously with such spiky flowers as gasplant, snapdragon, stock and gayfeather.

Snapdragons form the triangle, iris fill the pocket for this informal Moribana-style arrangement.

Although the snapdragon spikes give an illusion of height to the design, it is still low enough for use on a dining-room table, with some slight modifications of the basic design: place additional iris in the same fashion as those you can see on the other side of the arrangement. In this way, each diner will have an equally appealing view of the flowers.

The glaze lining of the shallow container picks up the color of yellow iris. A small touch, such as this, adds interest and finished appearance to the arrangement, as do the dark stones which disguise the needle point and base of stems.

For variety, always try to include some buds with the fully-open flowers in your arrangements of bearded iris.

Fill the pocket left in the center of this all-iris design with four bronzy-purple ones. (Or use any dark color for contrast with the paler varieties you have used.)

Cut the last stem of dark-toned iris shortest of all and insert it at center front. Face the bloom directly forward and allow it to project out over the container rim.

Iris arrangements are enhanced by the inclusion of some iris foliage, though care should be exercised to leave sufficient spring foliage so the plant can build up strength during summer to produce bloom for the following season.

In arranging iris, two rules followed by classical Japanese arrangers may be helpful: never set the blade edge of leaves to face the viewer; in any group of 2 or more leaves, place them so their tips curve inward, toward each other, and toward the flower which they accompany.

Flag iris, in sharply contrasting color, are ideal partners for peonies. Used to add height, they are placed behind the peonies.

Five blooms were chosen carefully to represent stages in development—from part- to fully-open. Largest bloom is placed low and forward, as a focal point in a flower composition designed to be seen from the front.

Peonies are early summer stars

Peonies have such enormous blooms that they demand strong companions, sturdy containers. Lilac branches and bearded iris offer excellent contrast of color and form, hold their own well in mixed arrangements such as those shown here.

Or, use a waxy peony by itself, with its own foliage—as in the arrangement of just one bloom across the page—simple and satisfying where space is limited.

Cut peonies at any time after color shows in buds and until they reach a fully open stage. Of course, they last longer if not full bloom when cut. Condition by splitting stem ends and plunging into deep water.

Maximum effect gained with minimum of material is always a challenge to arrangers.

Here's what you can do with one pastel-pink Chinese tree peony and just five of its own deeply notched leaves.

To duplicate this simple but arresting design, place small needle-point holder in the bottom of your container and secure it with florists' clay. Next, anchor the peony on it, slanting the bloom slightly toward the right side.

Now you're ready to insert the foliage. Select and place leaves so that they will form a triangular frame for one perfect bloom. The flower will help to hold foliage in place if leaf stems are too short to insert in the needle point.

Color and form of a rounded blue-green pottery container are well chosen as harmonious contrast for the delicate pink of the bloom and the lacy outlines of the peony foliage.

When you need a big, dramatic arrangement to place on the floor, combine peonies with soaring branches of lilac

Late spring or early summer—when peonies and lilacs bloom—is a favorite time for weddings. An arrangement like this one (or make it one of a pair) would be an impressive altar decoration. It would be handsome on any occasion, set on the floor, with plenty of free space surrounding it.

Use a heavy bronze or pottery container, preferably in some dark color, to give a visual sense of solidity, avoid any feeling of top-heaviness in design.

In this arrangement, two lilac branches, one lavender, one white, form two points of a triangle. Its third point is established by part-open peony at lowest point on the right. Center pocket was filled with 14 more peonies, each stem cut to a slightly different length and placed at an angle that separates it from its neighbors.

Summer's spirit

Summer's free and easy mood, her fullness, color and generally extravagant ways ought to inspire us when we design arrangements appropriate to this luxuriant season.

There's more than one way to symbolize summertime at her height. Most obvious, of course, are the generous effects we can achieve in mass arrangements such as the romantic centerpiece pictured below that are reminiscent of nature at her most lavish.

Another more subtle way to capture early summer's spirit with flowers is to emphasize the informal curves and spreading lines characteristic of midsummer growth, as in the arrangement at left. The shape of summer is quite different from the spear forms that denote spring, or the sparse, thin outlines most typical of autumn.

Arching branches of crab-apple form a triangular frame for a cluster of single peony blooms, poppies, and late purple iris. The leafiness of this arrangement makes it typical of summertime, in contrast to spring when bloom precedes leaf.

*Poppies last well in
an arrangement if their
stems are seared
at the time they're cut*

Fragile-looking poppies, with paper-thin petals, *can* be used successfully in arrangements if you treat them properly at the time you pick them.

Cut them the night before bloom opens; sear stem ends immediately after cutting. Use a candle or gas flame to sear. This prevents sticky fluid in stems from escaping and thus keeps poppies from wilting. Condition overnight in water.

In this graceful arrangement, feathery meadow rue furnishes the background for the line design. Each poppy stem is cut to a different length, slanted to keep the blooms separate.

Field flowers in happy profusion remind us of the summer countryside, of ease and informality.

Assembled rather than arranged, this centerpiece is completely natural in feeling, with daisies, poppies and cornflowers lavishly combined to echo the generosity of the season.

Cornucopia vase, with coy shepherdess and lamb, sets a tone of studied informality in the French fashion for this romantic early summer bouquet.

Wild penstemon forms tall background lines that frame a tight grouping of meadow rue, columbine, primroses in many colors, and a few floribunda fairy roses above the shepherdess' head.

Styles in roses—formal or informal

Roses respond well to use in either mass or line arrangements. As a rule, emphasis on line will result in a more informal appearance. Mass effects are generally more formal in character. These arrangements are good examples of two quite different styles, and they demonstrate convincingly the versatility and adaptability of roses.

In the design with roses below, the massing of blooms in an appropriate footed container and a low setting—produces a stately looking arrangement.

Across the page you see roses placed so that their stem lines are emphasized, in a low, pottery container. The impression is totally different, though equally agreeable. This informal, Moribana-style design would be at home in any modern room setting where simplicity is preferred.

Foliage to use with roses

The bloom of a rose is very strong competition and is best in combination with its own leaves or other boldly formed foliage. Avoid asparagus fern or other too delicate foliage.

Pine, fir, spruce, yew and most broadleaf evergreens make good rose partners.

Flowers that combine well with roses include the spiky stalks of delphinium, snapdragons, larkspur and buddleia.

In whatever way you arrange roses, remove lower leaves always and cut across stems diagonally for maximum water intake.

In a formal setting, roses combined with heather and a strikingly patterned foliage are compatible

Variegated pittosporum foliage, with its attractive whorl-shaped leaves, is placed to form a triangular background for this large-scale arrangement with an appealing, old-fashioned air. Roses that are nearly full-blown are the attention-getting focal point of the composition.

Sprigs of California heather introduce a welcome spiky contrast to the predominantly round forms of both blooms and foliage.

Snow-in-summer (*Cerastium tomentosum*) is a possible alternative to the variegated pittosporum. Or you might use any bold-leaved varieties of the broadleaf evergreen family to which pittosporum belongs. Camellia, laurel, or some of the hollies would be effective.

Large, footed china bowl is given additional height by being set onto a pedestal. Dainty china sheperdess placed nearby advances the theme of old-fashioned charm which makes the arrangement appear so well-suited to traditional room settings.

Two Tawny Gold and one New Yorker rose establish main lines. Tallest stem (a bud is best) is 1½ times container length.

Add four yellow, half-opened blooms cut to varying lengths. Place each one at a gentle slant around center blooms, as pictured.

Complete the arrangement by adding four more practically full-blown red roses. Cut each stem to a different length and place so each rose has a space to itself, does not appear crowded in with the others.

If you grow roses, a two-color arrangement of this kind offers you a good way to use what your garden affords on a single day.

Notice that the container is neutral, gray-green on its outer surface, yellow inside, in a color which is close to the Tawny Gold variety of rose. For brilliant flower combinations, container should be neutral.

A line-design with roses, arranged in Moribana style, uses branches of pine as Heaven and Man lines, with roses curving outward at right in the Earth line. White snapdragons make a fresh transitional note between pine branches and roses.

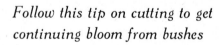

Follow this tip on cutting to get continuing bloom from bushes

When you cut roses, do it with the thought of leaving some buds to come later as well as the health of the bush.

Cut no longer a stem than necessary—some of the short stemmed roses are needed in most arrangements, anyway.

Leave at least two leaves of five leaflets each below the point where you make a cut. New buds will form in axils of leaves left on.

Just three roses are all you need to duplicate this simple but satisfying arrangement. The tallest stem should extend above the vase or pitcher rim at least 1½ times the container's height. Stagger the two shorter stems so they form a triangle.

Roses will last longer if you snip stems to the desired length while under water. This prevents air blocking the minute channels through which water rises in the stems.

Everyone's favorite flower is always in season

Capture the heady perfume of summer in a bouquet of roses—no matter what the time of year. They're America's favorite flower, and you can have them any time from your florist, as well as from your summer garden.

Just because the desire to smell a rose is universal and irresistible, try to place the arrangement where all can indulge and so reward the sense of smell as well as the eye.

Roses are resplendent in line arrangements accompanied by nothing more than their own foliage. And they're also magnificent when massed and combined with spiky or feathery stalks of such plants as delphinium, snapdragon, larkspur, buddleia. Or see how effective are the pine branches used with roses in the arrangement at far left.

Is there a "right" container?

The old theory that roses, a "fine" flower, *must* be placed only in crystal or silver containers has been exploded. Let the degree of formality you want help in choosing a container for your arrangement of roses.

Dainty garnet roses, available all year around from your florist, make appealing one-flower arrangements with their glossy foliage

Miniature in scale (compare the height of the arrangement with the coffeepot in the background) garnet or sweetheart roses are available in several shades, ranging from the palest shell pink through very dark red. Arranged in this fashion, they would grace a coffee table set for morning or after-dinner coffee with guests. Topped by a bud, the design places largest, fully open flowers lowest.

A romantic effect inspired by the cupid-borne porcelain bowl results from combining full-blown garden roses with airy sprays of baby's breath and blue spikes of larkspur. An echo of summer's most exuberant moods, this arrangement was designed by Mrs. Nelson Urban.

Lilies are proud summer beauties

Lilies, striking in form and color, and long-lasting in arrangements, are perfect subjects for the designer's art.

Not too many years ago, lilies other than the tawny tiger lily were a garden rarity. But the amazingly hardy and lovely hybrids recently developed in this country make today's lilies a favorite flower for summer arrangements, whether alone or in combination with other flowers and foliage, from late May into early September.

The pictured arrangements are evidence that lilies may be placed either high or low to good effect when they are featured in a mixed bouquet. And in both cases, it is desirable to include buds for contrast in form with the fully opened blooms.

When cutting lilies to use in arranging, do not remove more than a third of the total stem length. Only through foliage left on the stem, is the bulb able to build up the strength to form next year's bloom.

Happily paired are tiger lilies and fruited branches of Highbush Cranberry (*Viburnum Trilobum*) whose berries are just beginning to show color in an arrangement by Mrs. Merrill Cook.

Giving structure and form to the design are an interesting piece of driftwood and a large walnut plaque on which the arrangement is based. Both flower and foliage stems are secured in a cupholder obscured by leaf and bloom.

The appeal of a lily's remarkable waxiness is heightened when it is set off by flowers or foliage that appear velvety or dull by contrast.

Spikes of blue delphinium combined with white madonna lilies make a cool, serene summer arrangement. The metallic-blue and copper-green container is Japanese pottery, as distinguished in quality as the flowers it holds.

Form the triangular background with delphinium by trimming the tallest stalk to about twice the diameter of the bowl and placing it at the rear of a large needle-point holder. Cut a second stalk three-fourths the length of the first and slant it slightly to the right. Fill in the design with additional stems of varying length slanted to right and left.

Place lilies to form a second, lower triangle, letting one budded stem project forward from the bowl's rim. For contrast of form and weight at the base of a composition, lilies are a good choice to pair with delphinium, especially since several varieties of lilies are in flower at about the same time as the first of the delphinium spikes.

Pair lilies with other garden flowers which are in bloom at the same time to achieve creative color combinations that are in harmony with furnishings

Everyday zinnias are skillfully combined with lovely red-flecked lilies (*speciosum rubrum*) for an effect that's unorthodox but satisfying.

These delicately recurved lilies, buds as well as fully open flowers, form an airy background for the big, round form of the zinnias. The tallest lily stem is cut two-and-one-half times the length of bowl. Second lily and long-stemmed zinnia create the basic triangle, filled in at center.

Zinnias in shades of red, rose, and white echo the colors of the lilies. Two smaller white ones reaching far out to the right balance the height of tall lily stalks in background.

If your reasons for making unusual flower combinations are sound, by all means follow your impulse. There are no unbreakable rules in arranging. That's why we consider it to be an art and not a science.

A salute to the Early American era is offered by a contemporary arrangement in a white ironstone pitcher. Mixed flowers including stock, anemones, snapdragons, chartreuse spikes of bells of Ireland and Easter lilies are assembled in what appears at first to be an almost casual way. On second inspection, it is apparent that there is a careful design: lilies are featured by being placed both high and low; deep colors are largely grouped at the base; pale ones are used for upper outlines.

Everyday beauty with lilies

The appeal of the lily is legendary. Its beauty has inspired mankind for as long as there are written records to tell us so.

In their wild form, lilies are difficult to grow out of their native surroundings and so were long relatively unknown as a garden flower. But today's hybrids have made them easily available—to grow in your garden, or to buy as cut flowers from your florist during many months of the year.

Use lilies alone, add other garden foliage to fill out a design, or place them in joyously full mixed arrangements. Wherever you put them, the waxy sheen and perfect form of lilies will lift your spirits.

Regal lilies, their unopened buds showing color, are a favorite for midsummer arrangements. Sculptured-looking hosta foliage is combined with the lilies to add breadth and weight at the base of the arrangement. Flowers are placed with their trumpets facing in various directions so that the design will be equally attractive from all sides.

Foliage of fancy-leaf caladium, veined in shades of red, green and white, would also be attractive if similarly combined with white lilies.

Enchantment's vibrant orange is cooled by a froth of elderberry bloom

Reinforcing and harmonizing with the wall color in an entrance hall, three stems of Jan de Graff's popular hybrid lily, Enchantment, look regal in a mist of elderberry bloom.

An especially appropriate container is a Japanese usubata of bronze whose subdued sheen sets off glowing tones of the flowers.

Since it is important (for the sake of next year's bloom) not to cut more than a third of a lily's stem away with bloom, it is advantageous to combine lilies with some tall material—such as the elderberry branches—whenever height is needed in a finished arrangement. This design is by Mrs. Nelson Urban.

Imitate nature's flowing lines

July and August, most verdant months of the year, reveal nature's curving growth patterns, luxuriantly full, appealingly careless. In midsummer arrangements of garden flowers, you can pay no better tribute to the season than to reflect these lines in your designs.

You can bring the summer mood indoors with such unpretentious garden flowers as petunias, nasturtiums, zinnias and morning-glories arranged in easy fashion, with generous fullness.

When you go to the garden, stop a moment to search out nature's lines. Observe the direction of vine tips and tendrils, the angles at which leaves grow, the position of buds.

As you design your arrangement, remember all you have seen. You will not be copying nature exactly. Rather you will be doing what great Japanese arrangers have always attempted: expressing the ideal that exists in your mind.

Petunias are so plentiful all summer long that you won't mind cutting some. They're an informal flower and look best when they're arranged in a natural fashion that simulates patterns of growth.

Tallest stem is two and one-half times the height of the pitcher; it is placed at center back. Next tallest stems curve to right and left of main line.

The shorter-stemmed bloom serves as filler for the "holes." Flowers of closely related colors make the most pleasing group.

The vivid oranges, golds and scarlets of nasturtiums have a perfect foil in their own gray-green foliage. Use it freely.

Include buds among the wide-open blooms. They will open indoors, keep your arrangement interesting longer.

You can gain height and width for your composition by twining longer nasturtium stems around sticks and securing with bits of florists' tape. Place these as tall back and right horizontal lines. Group short stems at the center.

*The informality of basket containers
suits the mood of
easygoing summer arrangements*

Hang a pretty basket from your porch or patio roof and fill it with a profusion of whatever's blooming most freely at the moment.

We used zinnias, marigolds, celosia and brown-eyed susans for our July beauty. But you could compose a similar picture of September asters, goldenrod and chrysanthemums. Or, earlier, a mass of daisies, geraniums and ageratum would be a happy combination.

Mechanics are simple. To avoid too great a weight which might break the basket's chains, use saturated foam instead of a heavy bowl filled with water and a needle-point container. Wrap the block of foam in dark green foil (like the kind florists wrap gift pots in) to hold moisture in and obscure the foam from view.

Long trailing vines and scattered bloom of morning glories form a graceful silhouette in an informal arrangement of Nageire style. Especially appropriate is the basket container of Japanese origin, which balances the height and length of long tendrils that reach upward, and sweep down in a curving line onto the table top.

Each bloom lasts only for the day, but if you cut vines that have buds as well as open blooms, the buds will continue to open indoors.

Before you begin arranging morning-glories, char the ends of the vines over a low flame and plunge into cold water to condition for an hour or so.

Use pieces of stick or branches as supports for the lines you want. Secure the stems in a ball of crumpled chicken wire inside basket's glass liner.

For versatility, try the day lily

Day lilies bloom for only one day. They close at night. But don't let this quirk frighten you. Use them in daytime arrangements and cut stems with buds to open on the following day. They are as attractive when combined with other garden flowers as they are in arrangements of day lilies only.

Two stems of Golden Triangle day lily offer stunning contrast with the green glass bottle in which they are arranged. If day lily's own foliage is too limp, try iris spears.

To finish out the composition, Venetian glass fruit is arranged on a yellow glass plate, garnished with sprigs of geranium and begonia foliage. Water in the plate keeps them fresh.

Burnished copper pitcher vase is in perfect harmony with the color of rich apricot day lilies and bloom of wild butterfly weed in an informal arrangement of mixed flowers.

To give height to the composition, a nicely budded spray of clematis vine was inserted at center rear. Day lilies and clusters of butterfly weed are the focal point of the design.

Generous use of foliage makes two stalks of day lilies seem important.

A frosty glass bottle container strikes a refreshingly cool note that's welcome in all summertime arrangements.

Day lilies bloom so prolifically most of the summer that if you grow a few plants you need never be without an arrangement such as this to add color to your home. New varieties come in pinks, roses, and several shades of red.

Persian blue glass pitcher (directly below) is a flattering container for a casual grouping of annual larkspur, blue and white, and true lilies plus day lilies (*hemerocallis*).

You'll discover that mixed arrangements like this one gain in smartness, have a better designed appearance if you group flowers by variety instead of dotting them haphazardly.

If your pitcher is clear glass and you'd like to try out our color harmony, experiment with vegetable dyes to color the water.

Patio bouquet of day lilies (below, right) includes plenty of buds. Each day, as new buds open, faded flowers should be clipped away.

Cut sprays of different lengths, let some curve to right and left of tallest central stem line to give interest and variety to your arrangement. Include foliage for contrast.

Tall slender container is a Mexican water bottle, decoratively trimmed in raffia wrappings. It suits both the outdoor setting and the informal character of the arrangement.

View from both sides arrangement is lovely from all angles, the right accent for your dining room table or on a coffee table.

A triangular design is established with longer, budded stems of marigolds. Buds offer welcome contrast to the round form of fully open bloom.

Use a stem that is at least 1½ times the width of container as tallest line. Use shortest stems with largest flowers for filling the center of design.

Turn it around, and you'll see the arrangement in a glass basket is as attractive on this side as it was on the other. Bloom of five orange zinnias has been substituted for marigolds at the focal point of the design, though marigolds could have been used on both sides.

Lacy foliage of marigolds was carefully pruned so that what remains provides needed contrast in both color and shape.

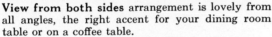

Tall vase of modern design has an interesting glaze that harmonizes with copper tones of Yellow Climax and Toreador varieties of marigolds (opposite).

To add sophistication, most marigold foliage was pruned away and branches of podocarpus used instead for fresh, green accent.

Branches of yew or pine could be combined with marigolds in a similar way.

Miniature bouquet of French marigolds in a tiny round bowl is just right in scale to brighten someone's breakfast tray.

Or vary your pattern of a centerpiece for a luncheon party by making several arrangements like this —one to set in front of each guest's place. An individual custard cup is about the right size and could be used as a container.

Make sure design is attractive on both sides.

New stylishness for marigolds

It's easy to take marigolds for granted just because they're so plentiful. Don't do it. They can be the flower arranger's best friends, not only because they're in bloom all season but because they mimic other blooms—carnations and chrysanthemums —so well in size and texture.

Take advantage of tall budded stems to arrange line designs that get away from the stereotype of a bowlful of marigolds. Don't hesitate to prune foliage, using it only for accents. Or try combining marigolds with a more exotic foliage to lend them a newly stylish appearance.

Zinnias, brilliant as the trimmings of a Mexican fiesta, are a gift to us from that sunny south-of-the-border land.

Starting from the original Mexican wildlings, hybridizers have developed varieties in a seemingly endless range of sizes and vivid hues. An easy-to-grow annual, zinnias should be a summer stand-by in every flower arranger's cutting garden.

You'll make the most of the zinnia's appealingly primitive nature—bright hues, rough texture—if you choose suitably strong containers of wood, pottery, or metal in the group of neutral or earth colors.

In a neutral setting that needs an accent, you'll be sure of a stand-out with an arrangement of these flowers. Or, to reinforce a more colorful scheme, you're almost certain to find some zinnia colors that will harmonize perfectly with your room furnishings.

Play up the bold colors of zinnias

Branches of crab apple, their fruits just beginning to show color, rise high above grouped zinnias, arranged so they will be attractive from all angles when placed on a low table.

Cut branches of crab apple the day before you plan to make this arrangement, pound bottom two inches of the stems, scrape away bark, and plunge branches into a pail of water to condition.

Use a big, heavy needle point to support the weight of branches. Fashion a triangular frame for the flowers. Tallest branch is more than two times the width of shallow, rectangular container.

Place the zinnias low in the arrangement, inserting each stem at a different angle, and varying the stems in length. Turn the container about as you work so both sides will be equally effective and well filled in.

Line design of zinnias in a horn-shaped ceramic container places the more diminutive varieties, Tom Thumb and Persian Carpet, in a sweeping, descending curve that ends with a bud.

Flowers were thoroughly conditioned in advance, so stems would be strong enough to hold the wanted positions in the arrangement.

Sansevieria spears establish height in a vertical design featuring deep-toned (Dark Jewel) zinnias.

Globe thistle heads make a smooth transition between zinnias and sansevieria, with variegated coleus foliage giving finish at the bottom.

Experiment with line designs that feature zinnias in one-flower arrangements, or combined with green foliage of other plants

The strap-shaped foliage of Ismene, or Peruvian daffodil, forms a half-fan background for an arrangement of Oriole and Fire Flame zinnias. Balancing the background height, hosta foliage extends forward at lower right.

Flowers within the central composition are grouped by colors to gain a much more sophisticated effect than could be obtained were the zinnias placed haphazardly.

A gray-green metal usubata of contemporary design is congenial in both color and style to a modern line-and-mass arrangement. Displayed on a console table, the flowers are a decorative accent for an entrance hall, their vibrance in contrast to the subdued tones of wood paneling.

All three of the arrangements on this page, featuring zinnias in modern compositions, were designed by Mrs. Merrill Cook.

Sketch bold line designs using gladiolus

Never out of season, gladiolus are one of the few flowers you can count on using in arrangements twelve months of the year. If they're not available from your garden, the florist can oblige with shipped-in beauties. Another virtue of gladiolus is that—in the right container and location—you can get good effects with only a few stalks. When you need a dramatically large-scale design, they're equally obliging.

It pays, therefore, to experiment with gladiolus arrangements until you've worked out favorites that are satisfying in particular locations in your home. Face them right or left according to the demands of the situation. You'll enjoy repeating them, varying the size and color according to the flowers that are available.

When you buy gladiolus, hunt for stalks that include fresh-looking foliage. Let nature help you obtain a satisfying design by supplying you with built-in contrasts of round and spear shapes.

If you grow gladiolus, cut them when the second floret is ready to open. Recut each stem just as you place it in deep water to condition before arranging.

To avoid having all stiff, straight stems, lean some slantwise during the conditioning, encouraging them to assume a slight curve. Remove bud tips, unless you need them for height, as they seldom open.

Tall jardiniere and a full arrangement of gladiolus will decorate a large space.

Brilliant orange-red gladiolus massed in Oriental style are a particularly effective selection for a contemporary room decorated with today's Orient-inspired home furnishings and accessories.

For an arrangement as large as this one, you will need a dozen or more stalks of gladiolus. Choose the longest stems available, and be sure to include a spear or two of foliage with each one.

If none of the stems is as long as the one you need for the Heaven line, lengthen by taping on a portion of stem removed from another. Just be sure original stem is still long enough to reach water.

Before you begin your arrangement, snap off undeveloped buds. Place a 24-inch stem of gladiolus in slightly off-center position in a 12- to 14-inch long bowl. Slant 16-inch spike to your right, an 8-inch one toward your left shoulder for Man and Earth lines.

Place 14-inch gladiolus stem just to the left of the tall center stalk, disguising its bare stem; put a 7-inch stem low at center, projecting forward over the edge of container. Add foliage spears to each gladiolus spike, letting leaves follow the angles of flowers.

*This arranging formula
always yields
a pleasing composition*

Finish off your design by adding two more stems: place a 20-inch gladiolus to right rear of tallest stem, giving an illusion of depth; add an 18-inch stem in front of the tallest spike. Slant to left.

When arranging full spikes of gladiolus, don't overcrowd them. Let each ruffled flower have a space to itself.

With this type of Moribana arrangement, the low rectangular container has become as "basic" as a black dress in a woman's wardrobe. This irregularly striped one introduces contrast to vertical lines of arrangement, but a plain one may be used effectively.

Chrysanthemums— everyone's favorite for fall

Old Chinese prints often show the spider-form chrysanthemum in all its fragile beauty, informing us that the variety is indeed an ancient one.

To duplicate this arrangement, hold three "anchor" flowers in your hand to establish a major triangle. When their position suits you, wire the three stems together securely and insert in vase.

Steady these basic stems with your left hand as you insert filler flowers with your right. Place so that each of the flower heads has a separate space.

Coral-red gladiolus, torch-like in shape, frame and flatter bi-color chrysanthemums with round, shaggy heads.

In a setting as subdued as this one, the double-color impact of intense blue bowl and brilliant flowers is a clever decorating accent. Impact and effectiveness of an arrangement are greatest when flower colors repeat those appearing elsewhere in a room's color scheme.

When gladiolus fade, refresh the arrangement by substituting big branches of pine as a frame for chrysanthemums.

Time-honored chrysanthemums were cultivated in China more than 2,000 years ago. The Japanese adopted the flower, developed it highly, and made it officially theirs by incorporating it in the crest and seal of the Mikados centuries ago. In Japan of today, it is the prescribed flower, with pine, for joyful New Year celebrations.

Chrysanthemums as cut flowers last so well that they're a deserved favorite for home arrangements. Cut stems to the lengths you want in your design; pull off the leaves that will be under water. Crush the ends of woody stems with a hammer, so flowers will get ample water easily.

The trouble you take with this extra treatment will be repaid by the surprisingly long period the flowers stay fresh, especially those of the small pompon variety, like the yellow ones just below.

Let the type of chrysanthemum to be arranged be a deciding factor in selecting an appropriate design and container. The giant mop heads won't take to the same style of arrangement as the button tips that are so appealing in the mass composition at right. But they will lend themselves well to combinations with material of contrasting form, such as the torch-shaped gladiolus with which they are so effectively grouped at left.

Victorian in style and opulent in looks is a mass arrangement of pink and mauve button chrysanthemums combined with dahlias of related colors. Nestled in its Vieux Paris porcelain basket, the bouquet recalls the elegance of turn - of - the - century manners and fashions.

Keep the mirror view in mind when you design for such placement.

Button tips show to good advantage in Moribana style line design.

One prerequisite to success with an arrangement such as this is an ample supply of fresh-looking foliage. Wilted leaves or bare stems will ruin the effect.

Establish main lines first with tallest stems and then add flowers to fill in central area.

Weeds, grasses and slim cattails like those in this arrangement can be found on the banks of ponds, lakes, and marshes almost everywhere.

Fill your husband's fishing creel with your discoveries and set it on the end of the dining table the next time he brings home a catch of fish.

Gather autumn's offerings in woods and fields

Autumn, when the bloom in your garden may be sparse, is the time to open your eyes to new materials for arrangements.

Explore the woods and roadsides. You'll discover many kinds of vines of unusual appeal, seed pods, weeds and grasses useful in seasonal arrangements because of their decorative shapes, colors, textures.

Milkweed pods, sumac, pine cones, oats, goldenrod, and a world of others besides the ones pictured here are ready to add interest to fall arrangements.

To supplement your harvest, inspect your florist's treasury of exotic dried materials such as wood roses from Hawaii, palm spathes, and lotus seed pods.

Subtle, monochromatic arrangement of dried materials makes up in textural and compositional interest for any lack of brilliance in color.

Begin with two bunches of dried material—common dock would work well—placed right and center. Insert a few stems of dried cockscomb on a slant to your left, as in the first of the two small pictures below. (Wiring each bunch together before you place it insures a stable finished design.)

In the upper middle section (see second picture below) we placed two full stalks of bleached milkweed pods, then artichoke seed pods a little lower, and seven spears of wheat. Lower focal point is of five stems of dried Bells of Ireland.

Used as "helpers" are a few cattails, some stems of teasel and a little glycerin-treated foliage.

Rich, brown wood tones of a highly polished burl base contrast attractively with paler autumnal colors of a fruit and vegetable decoration designed for an informal luncheon or a fall supper party.

Sprouted onion and scrubbed carrots are amusing additions to an edible centerpiece—peppers, grapes, squash—but are so unpretentious that they should not be included if the occasion is at all formal.

A pine branch, secured in a needle-point holder that is hidden by placement of vegetables, gives height and added interest to an arrangement which was designed to be seen from front.

Bittersweet's interesting orange and red berries and curving tendrils make it an obvious choice for an early autumn arrangement.

In a wall container, use it as it grows, keeping your design sharply etched with graceful high and low lines by pruning branches to eliminate any conflicting side shoots from the main stems. Cluster short pieces at the center of the design.

Sweet Autumn clematis is another good vine to use in a wall arrangement. Clip a few sprays and place them in a shellacked gourd like this, or in any other container of harmonious color.

Place the clippings of vine so that some will reach upward, others trail down naturally. They are stiff enough so they will hold their positions without need of additional propping for stability.

Dried arrangements take to tall vases

The tall vases which are now in vogue as decorative room accessories offer a real challenge to the flower arranger. Highly dramatic in appearance, they demand exotic arrangements, as flamboyant in character as they are themselves.

Dried arrangements meet the requirements, and are long-lasting enough to warrant the time—or money—it takes to assemble the necessary materials. Easily available is a wide choice of grasses, seed heads, and pods with the long stems you need to balance the height of the container.

In choosing a tall vase to decorate your home, consider both room color scheme and the amount of space available.

Vases of colors that repeat one or more hues in a well-defined room scheme are effective, but they limit flower and foliage choices to those that harmonize. Neutral vase colors allow the widest possible color choice in plant materials.

A tall vase of large diameter must have ample space if it is to be a decorative success. If it is too big for its setting, it will look uncomfortably crowded; if it is too small, it will seem insignificant.

Colorful vases
complement
neutral foliage tones

Slender pottery cylinder, decorated with horizontal bands of color, confers new importance on a sheaf of dried grasses, bells of Ireland, magnolia leaves, and an artichoke bud.

If tallest stems available are shorter than you need, use florists' tape to fasten them onto sticks that will extend their height.

The fireplace wall is a congenial background for a sleek gray cat vase filled with a casual arrangement of marsh grasses, cattails, milkweed pods, and a few bright sprays of bittersweet.

A polished wood base like the one used with this arrangement is, of course, optional. But it does add a trim finish, increase the visual balance.

For entrance hall drama, take one Ali Baba jar; fill with tall dried desert plants, lotus seed pods and foliage, trailing stems of bittersweet vine that reach nearly to the floor.

Place your dried arrangement where it flanks the front door and will be admired by all arriving guests during the fall and early winter.

The fruits of autumn are rich in color

Autumn, the harvest season, offers a gorgeous array of berried and fruited branches for the arranger's art.

Some, like bittersweet, will dry and hold their color indefinitely. Others, if kept in water, will retain freshness for a number of weeks.

When you cut branches, look for some with natural curves to help establish the primary outlines of your arrangement. Then, prune judiciously to emphasize nature's satisfying patterns.

The shorter, straighter stems can be used to good advantage when you want to fill in the center of your design.

Berried branches make memorable arrangements whether they are used alone or in combination with flowers. In mixed arrangements, they have the happy faculty of making a handful of flowers look like more.

Daisy chrysanthemums serve as helpers for the main outlines of the arrangement and to fill in the open spaces left between cockscomb and asters. Their smaller form and finer texture make an attractive transition between the fragility of the branches and the bold form of cockscomb and asters.

The elegance of a gilt metal usubata serving as container confers a formal air on the arrangement.

Main outlines of this autumn arrangement are established with three branches of ornamental crab apple. (See Step I at left for placement.) Add two stems of cockscomb.

Step II (at right) shows positions for the insertion of three more stems of cockscomb, placed low, as a focal point. In triangular formation, add three purple asters.

Hedge apples or Osage oranges, their nubby skins a true chartreuse in color, are the attention-getting feature in this combination with short branches of pine and curving, fruited twigs of a bittersweet vine.

A needle point was used to secure stems of both pine and bittersweet; one of the Osage oranges rests on it, hides it from view.

No water is necessary for arrangements of these materials which will stay fresh several weeks without it.

A triangular design for a low bowl places stems of berried viburnum (Highbush Cranberry) in the Heaven, Man, and Earth positions to establish the height and breadth of the arrangement.

The pleasing effect gained by the use of branches longer than those conventionally recommended (tallest branch 2 or 3 times the length or breadth of the container) is proof that rules are guides for beginners, not restrictions on skilled arrangers.

Masses of short-stemmed chrysanthemums in autumn's golds and bronzes harmonize with the colorful berries and fill in the central portion of the composition. A few chrysanthemums project forward, furthering a three-dimensional feeling.

Firethorn's red glow is enhanced by the patina of a polished Chinese pewter container, its lid placed nearby to become a part of the total composition.

Inspired by, but not adhering closely to Oriental three-point style, the design is roughly triangular in its outlines.

The central cluster, with no foliage showing, is composed of holly berries.

Scarlet coat of mounted soldier in porcelain figure imitates the brilliant color of berries and establishes its relationship to the grouping, although it is not of Oriental design.

This full arrangement, on an antique chest, was seen at a "Tradition in Flowers and Furnishings" show presented by the Evanston Garden Club.

Dry flowers and foliage for a colorful winter bouquet

Fresh flowers and greens—such as goldenrod, strawflowers, cockscomb, oats, rye, leaves, seed pods, and ferns—can be dried for rich winter bouquets. You need no special equipment. A closet or your attic can serve as the "drying room" and some of the loveliest materials are found growing wild. Mrs. Louise B. Fisher of Williamsburg, Virginia, designed the arrangements shown on these pages and devised the drying instructions we include as well.

Timing is important in the gathering of materials. Cut flowers in semi-bud form. They'll open into full bloom as they dry.

Gather grasses and ferns in the morning, when they are fresh. Cut leaves as they start turning from green to yellow to red. Select flat branches of foliage for ease in pressing them effectively.

Put all fresh materials in buckets of water as they're cut if you have to transport them any distance. The sooner you press colored materials after picking, the brighter they'll stay during the drying process.

Choose a dark, dry location, as dampness prevents proper drying and light fades colors. If rodents are a problem, set out mothballs to protect seedheads from them.

Memories of summer can be kept alive in an arrangement of dried foliage, ferns, grasses, and flowers

Colorful bouquet contains dried materials only—yellow and rose strawflowers, grasses, beech leaves, fern fronds, honesty, and pearly everlasting.

Arranged in the traditional Williamsburg manner, the massive background is composed entirely of foliages, with central interest provided by the cluster of strawflowers.

Dried materials are ready to use in arrangements when flower petals feel rigid and no moisture is left by the paper layers of pressed foliage. If not thoroughly dry when you remove them from your presses, leaves will curl, lose their shape. Under proper conditions, drying takes 3 to 4 weeks.

To press leaves, lay each branch out carefully between layers of paper on a flat surface—floor or table. Make as many layers as you like. Weight down the pile with books, suitcases, or any heavy objects.

Another way to treat foliage is to slit branch ends, insert in several inches of a solution of equal parts water and glycerin. Let stand for several weeks.

To obtain curved stems for variety in arrangements, dry part of your tall grasses and weeds by placing upright in kegs, fruit jars, or milk bottles set on the floor of your drying room. Leave undisturbed for several weeks or until material is completely dry.

Unless you will use immediately, protect from dust by separating varieties and storing bunches in cartons.

For the straight stems you want on most materials, tie into bunches and string on lines hung at a height convenient for you to reach. Let dry 3 or 4 weeks.

Don't wait for fall to begin collecting. Many summer flowers such as larkspur, ageratum, globe amaranth, stock and zinnias will dry beautifully and hold their color. Cut and hang each variety when at its peak.

Gather colorful leaves and
heads of bloom to include in your
dry arrangements

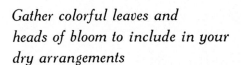

Absence of light during the drying period is essential if you want colorful materials to use in your dry arrangements. Once flowers and leaves are dry and colors have "set," they won't fade, even if you display the arrangement in a sunny location.

This bouquet combines beech leaves, red sage, goldenrod, cockscomb, golden celosia, blue sage, and pearly everlasting in colorful colonial style.

Among the other weeds and cultivated plants that will hold their color when dried are: astilbe, sumac, Joe-pye weed, yarrow, clover, statice, spirea, delphinium, vervain, tansy, salvia, beebalm, and butterfly weed.

Dry arrangements in colonial style

So colorful is this fan-shaped bouquet that it's hard to believe all its components are dry flowers and foliage. Included in the mixed arrangement are: strawflowers, celosia, Yorktown onions, blue larkspur, artemisia, scarlet sage, honesty, and maidenhair fern—all plants known to have flourished in the Virginia gardens or grown wild in the woodlands of the colonial period.

This arrangement, by Miss Edna Pennell, Flower Arranger for Colonial Williamsburg, was photographed in a bedroom of the Governor's Palace, on a bedside table of eighteenth century design.

The practiced arranger develops an ability to see beauty in every growing thing. Grasses, weeds, and pods the novice might reject as too prosaic to be used in flower arrangements are precious "finds" to those who have learned to look at nature with an appreciative awareness.

When we are able to do this, we are no different from our colonial forebears. In the Williamsburg of colonial days, winter bouquets were much admired. They were made of the various dried materials—both wild and cultivated—which grew in their gardens or in the nearby woodlands.

Today's visitors to the exhibition buildings of Restored Colonial Williamsburg may see winter bouquets exactly like the ones admired by the colonists. Their color and beauty are an inspiration to all of us to gather the materials and fashion our own bright bouquets for winter homes.

Festively full bouquet of dry materials is displayed in the formal dining room of the Governor's Palace at Williamsburg.

In accordance with the customs of eighteenth century colonists, flowers—dry or fresh—are always placed on chests or side tables, never on dining tables.

Miss Pennell, designer of this arrangement, used a fan of white poplar leaves as background for goldenrod, celosia, strawflowers, chaste tree, pearly everlasting.

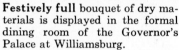

*Use traditional styles
for dry arrangements suited
to period furnishings*

Tones of brown predominate in a mixed arrangement of dried seed heads, branches, and berries.

The style of the bouquet and its ingredients are appropriate to a period setting: "brothers" desk, quaint Bristol green glass paperweight, glass study lamp, and the wall decorations of framed racing handkerchiefs and Early American prints of hunting scenes.

The arrangement was displayed at an exhibit arranged by the Garden Club of Evanston, Illinois.

Contrasting colors of red plum foliage (*Prunus Pissardii*) and gray-green Pfitzer juniper branches are mutually complementary in a simple all-foliage arrangement in a tall basket container.

You will find that arrangements using the darker colored foliages take on more drama when they are set against a light and unpatterned background, like this white fireplace mantel.

Plum foliage forms both Heaven and Man lines of a triangular Nageire arrangement, with juniper used for the Earth position in a design by Mrs. Tomoko Yamamoto.

Foliage alone has beauty and freshness

Nothing does more than cut green foliage to freshen up a room at minimum expenditure of both time and money.

Foliage arrangements have a natural affinity for modern furnishings and contemporary architecture. But they take to the traditional also, if they're styled properly and placed in a suitable container.

Foliage is easy to come by: explore the countryside or your own garden looking for branches of interesting form, foliage of many shapes and colors.

If you're an apartment dweller, or have a small garden with few shrubs and trees, get acquainted with your florist. He sells a wide variety of foliages and greens at modest prices. Almost all are so long lasting you'll feel your money's well spent.

To keep foliage of woody branches from wilting, be sure to treat them before arranging by pounding the ends, scraping off bark, and plunging in water to condition.

The iridescence of canna leaves is increased by the similar glaze of the pottery container.

Canna leaves are pliable and may be manipulated. To get leaves to curve to right and left, bend gently with both thumbs at the point where the leaf springs out of the stem.

When garden flowers are few, assemble a foliage-only arrangement with clippings from your shrubs, trees, and other garden plants.

To make it interesting, look for contrasting textures—shiny and dull; dark colors and light; feathery and solid leaf forms.

From a Southern garden, you might combine foliage of magnolia, papyrus, crinum, clippings from a begonia plant, and a few bud sprays from a rice-paper plant to obtain interesting contrasts.

This all-green foliage arrangement was designed by Mrs. Benjamin Clayton.

Foliage-only arrangements

When flowers in your garden are few, turn to the greens for foliage-only arrangements that will dramatize a bare wall or freshen a table top. Color is never a problem, since nature's greens are good with everything.

If you have no garden, your florist can oblige with a good assortment of handsome and inexpensive foliages so long-lasting you'll be well repaid by your modest investment in greens.

Some foliage—like the magnolia at left—is impressive enough to arrange without the addition of flowers or a contrasting leaf. Others, less dramatic in themselves, will be attractive in mixed arrangements that include two or more mutually complementary leaf forms, colors, patterns, and textures.

Magnolia leaves—rich, shiny green on one side and velvety bronze on the other—are especially effective in large-scale arrangements. Use them where you have a big wall to fill.

Cut four branches to assorted lengths, making the tallest one three times the height of your container. Place them in triangular position, with right and left branches pointing forward to each shoulder. Use the shortest branch at center.

Sansevieria foliage, mottled with cream, and glossy green rhododendron leaves secured on a needle-point holder combine to fashion a modern decoration for a desk or table top.

The unusual boat-shaped container is of black pottery with a beige-colored diagonal stripe as trim, and a raised base.

Possible substitutes for rhododendron leaves include: camellia, cherry laurel, loquat, holly, firethorn, pittosporum.

Three varieties of hosta foliage, two solid green, and one touched with white, are skillfully combined with colored coleus in a design by Mrs Merrill Cook.

The black Japanese pottery container is especially congenial because of its mottled trim which mimics the spatterlike patterns of the coleus foliage. For finish, the container was set on a base which is a circle of walnut.

Traditional styling and a silver urn container for an all-foliage arrangement make it completely suitable for a gracious period room setting.

Sedge, pittosporum, magnolia leaves were assembled in a fan-shaped design to decorate a Biedermeier commode in an entrance hall.

This arrangement was included in a show featuring tradition sponsored by the Evanston Garden Club.

Umbrella-shaped heads of wild parsnip weed, gone to seed in early summer, have fascinating form and stylish coloring that make them fit subjects for the arranger's art.

Their own leaves are attractive enough to be a suitable foil for the seed heads, though you may enjoy combining them with such garden foliage as hosta leaves, solid green or variegated.

A shining brass scale pan—like those once used in butcher shops—makes a tasteful container for a large-size informally styled arrangement. Branches were cut to different lengths and placed to show profiles as well as full-face views of the weeds in a design by Mrs. Nelson Urban.

A foam of meadow-rue (*Thalictrum*) (at left) is a splendid show-off in combination with spears of ornamental grass in a Nageire-style arrangement designed by Mrs. Fae Huttenlocher.

White, pink, and purple meadow-rue, more common than this yellow variety, grow in both wild and cultivated types that are handsome in perennial borders, but not often singled out as the stars of arrangements. Here's evidence meadow-rue deserves more attention than it usually gets.

Cut stems of meadow-rue to lengths in proportion to your container to establish Heaven, Man, and Earth lines. It's used here for Mountain and Meadow also. Fill in with spears of ornamental grass—or substitute iris foliage if you like.

Imaginative ways to use grasses, weeds, and wildflowers

To the gifted flower arranger, nothing is more stimulating than to discover new ways to use old, familiar weeds, leaves, or flowers. If you've never considered the plants featured here as potential materials for an arrangement, these three designs may help to convince you that they are well worth your attention in the future.

Spring, summer, autumn—each offer fresh choices of leaf and bloom. Make a jaunt to the countryside to see what's in season. Require yourself to put aside old prejudices and look at each plant with a fresh eye, ready to see beauty in common materials you have overlooked in the past.

In the case of wildflowers, of course, you won't pick them in parks and protected areas. But many, like goldenrod, hardy asters and wild parsnip are yours for the taking on a country roadside—weeds to the farmer, but fascinating plant material to the perceptive eye of an imaginative arranger.

Goldenrod and purple hardy single asters that grow on autumn roadsides in such profusion make a pretty pair in a miniature-scale arrangement. (The container is a Japanese rice bowl of the size that holds an individual serving.)

When you plan an expedition to gather weeds and wildflowers, carry a pail of water with you to keep them fresh until you reach home.

Chapter 4

Flowers can make your tables festive

Fresh flowers for the table! Just the phrase calls up a picture of hospitality, of food shared in a lighthearted mood, of pleasant occasions in the past when we have gathered, with family and friends, to enjoy one another's company in happy surroundings.

In the following pages we show you a wide variety of ways to use flowers and growing things as ornaments for festive tables. Some of the arrangements are formal; others are completely casual. But all—we trust—are designed to make the sharing of food a gracious occasion, not merely a concession to the human need to eat at regular intervals.

Tradition favors the symmetrical centerpiece, and it is a logical choice when the guests are to be seated at the sides of the table, host and hostess at the ends.

Flowers arranged in this fashion should be designed to be attractive from every angle, and the centerpiece should not be so tall as to obstruct across-the-table talk.

Some arrangers insist that flower centerpieces be no taller than nine inches above the table top. Such a rule, if it was ever valid, is now outmoded. Feathery tufts taller than this limit would certainly not interfere with guests' views. Nor would twin topiary arrangements separated by candles, like those pictured which were designed by Mrs. Theodore Stroud.

If you are in doubt about the height of your own centerpiece, sit down and test the across-the-table visibility. Let this decide, rather than a check with the ruler.

How to make topiaries

Form a ball of sphagnum moss; wrap and tie with string; soak thoroughly in water.

Remove gladiolus florets from stalk gently; using hairpin-like wires which florists call "picks," fasten the florets and camellia leaves to the ball of moss. Impale the ball securely on a ribbon-wrapped dowel.

Use florists' clay to secure needle-point holder in low bowl. Insert end of dowel in needle point; disguise with short stems of ivy and pittosporum, or any suitable greens.

118

Harvest theme employs colorful Indian corn and chrysanthemums in contrast to brown rim of pottery, matching braided straw mats.

Mixed nosegay of summer bloom is harmonious in style with dainty china pattern; repeats blue of linens, adds analogous rose.

Coordinating flowers and table settings

Think *color* first when you select the flowers, fruit, foliage or other decorative materials for the table. They may match, harmonize, or contrast with colors of china, linens, or glassware and still create a delightful effect.

But let it be clear that flower color is part of a considered scheme—not just a happenstance matter.

Reflect the seasons to get variety into table decorations. In spring, use the plentiful pastels; in autumn, turn to the richer, deeper hues.

Don't feel that everything must be an exact "match," but rather that it must "belong" to the ensemble.

Study the seven suggested settings pictured to see how we took flower cues from colors and patterns of linens and china. Borrow and adapt these schemes to suit your requirements.

To give you a hint of the variety that's attainable, we've set this table with two different sets of china—one patterned in a white base, the other in a solid color.

Notice that the same arrangement is equally effective with both sets of dishes, because it takes its color cue from golds that appear in the table linens.

Cornflowers and poppies echo a complementary color scheme stated by the linens and glass, give dash to white china. White flowers with orange or blue could also be used effectively with the same setting.

Analogous colors—neighbors on the color wheel—are high fashion. Here they're picked up from the pattern of the place mat, and repeated in an edible centerpiece of cherry tomatoes and oranges for a brunch table.

Mix-and-match table (it's a practical solution for occasions when a big crowd is expected) escapes a confused look by choosing related colors blue and green for linens, then uniting the entire scheme with the neutral colors of a fall fruit centerpiece.

Fruit decoration is keyed to both sets of pottery—harmonious in color with one, and matching the pattern of the other.

Basket container for the fruit states that this is an informal occasion—perhaps a family gathering for Thanksgiving.

The pattern of your dishes can be a good starting point for developing the color scheme for a table setting and the kind of centerpiece that decorates it.

Gray-green and purple are both flattering colors to use with a grape-patterned set of dishes, as we see from this diamond-shaped runner effect created by overlapping contrasting napkins.

The grape pattern is repeated in the decorations on glasses and in the fruit of a centerpiece anchored on the black-sprayed figure that serves as container.

Color is the key to pretty tables. It doesn't matter whether dishes are of china, pottery or melamine; whether you own sterling, silverplate or stainless steel; damask or straw mats; whether your centerpiece is of roses or radishes.

What counts is what you do with what you have to create an inviting table. See our accent-on-color settings for ideas to start you off on new schemes.

A bouquet of well-scrubbed radishes in a milk-glass goblet are vivid and inviting against a blue-green cloth.

Golden wheat in a lacquer bowl (upper right) harmonizes with oranges and browns of place mats; matches the color of bamboo napkin rings.

"Good morning" setting (center left) is all in blue and white, with a handful of fresh daisies to lift the spirits and whet morning appetites.

Another breakfast setting (at center right) looks more festive because of a few stems of variegated ivy and fragrant lily of the valley in a copper mug.

Something special (lower left), like a family birthday, might inspire you to use your best embroidered linen place mats and blue-and-gold-banded china. Tea roses and candles (three in a row if there's room) might march down the table in blue glass goblets.

Gala luncheon for the ladies (lower right) puts a single pink carnation and bits of huckleberry foliage in a beribboned goblet at each guest's place.

An all-blue-and-white dining area responds to an injection of bright red in the form of roses combined with white chrysanthemums for a centerpiece, and red straw place mats against a white table top.

Color cues to inviting tables

A rosy rooster was the inspiration for this appetizing breakfast-in-bed tray, carried out in a red-green scheme.

Two stems of meadowrue, full-blown pink rose, and several stems of red weigela placed low are arranged informally in an ash tray that doubles as a flower container. Flowers don't match the rooster exactly, but are in good harmony with it.

The handsomely designed, unadorned white china shows off to excellent advantage in the bright-colored setting, against a dark background. Deep blue or purple would be stylish alternates for the mat.

Single-color schemes—those using two or more shades of a single hue—like the pink and red on this dinner table—are an almost sure-fire way to obtain dramatic effects.

White snapdragons and green foliage introduce the needed amount of contrast.

Castilian candlesticks are ringed with garnet roses, trimmed with grapes for dramatic table decor.

Obscured by the roses, three flat 7-ounce cans, pierced near the rim and wired in place, hold water. Grapes were wired to the candlestick separately.

Ingenious containers for rose arrangements to set at either end of a buffet are two hurricane-style candleholders. Set cupholders in the base to secure flower stems. Make certain rose foliage disguises them.

Roses say that dinner is a special occasion

The natural elegance of the rose makes it a favorite flower for all festivities we consider truly special. And when we use roses lavishly, we say—without the need for words—"let us share in happy celebration of this joyful occasion."

If your group of guests is small, you will probably plan a traditional dinner, with guests seated and served by hosts or servants. For such a dinner, twin candlestick arrangements like those designed by Mrs. A. M. McLeod—one of the winners in a national table-setting contest—are regal table decorations.

If many guests are invited, you may decide to serve buffet style. In this case, plan a symmetrical centerpiece for each table, and set more flowers—perhaps arranged like those in the silver and glass candleholders at left—on the sideboard from which guests help themselves to food.

Music-loving friends will be enchanted by a salute to their interests in the form of four small ceramic musicians. A low centerpiece of pansies and daisies is keyed to the soft pink and lavender of lacy place mats and the unusual pattern of marbleized salad plates. Milk-glass goblets and white napkins relate to china.

Daisy-patterned china inspired this nicely coordinated setting for a ladies' luncheon party. An organdy overskirt for the tablecloth is trimmed with an applique of daisies, and these flowers, together with some spikes of snapdragon, reappear in the fresh yellow and white centerpiece which repeats the crisp color scheme.

Pink and orchid tea table is as romantic as an old-fashioned valentine greeting.

Quite in keeping is a fluted milk-glass bowl, lined in cranberry, to hold 12 pink and white carnations, with stems of freesia to give height at the center of the arrangement.

Happy birthday table—the same scheme could serve for other occasions, minus tablecloth trim—matches flowers and napkins to a colored border on the china.

Extra flowers taped to prettily wrapped gift packages become an attractive part of the setting.

Especially for the ladies

When your party is for ladies only, you may be as feminine as you please with flowers to make the occasion a charming one. It's your chance to use all the table setting ideas you have had to reject as too frilly for affairs that included men as well as women guests.

Let soft pastel tints, nosegay arrangements and dainty accents be the order of the day. Your women guests—whatever their ages—will be flattered, and you'll have fun with an occasional splurge of femininity.

If a word of caution is not out of order in a discussion of feminine table settings, perhaps it should be said that accessories are most effective when used with restraint. Don't scatter little ceramic figures about the table. Work them into a flower arrangement if you can do so cleverly. Otherwise, it will be best to omit them.

Bridge tables can be as invitingly set as your dining room table when your guest list is too long to seat everyone together.

Take a cue from the pattern of the cloth for choosing the kinds and colors of flowers. Arrange them in one of your goblets, and tie a ribbon onto an extra rose as a party favor for each of your guests to wear.

Avoid tall arrangements for bridge tables which are less steady than conventional dining tables. Use saturated foam to hold stems of flowers. This party table and the one below were designed by Mrs. F. W. Pickworth.

Use feminine colors when you set your table for social gatherings of women friends

Happy the bride-to-be who is feted at so charming a table as this! Its centerpiece mimics the bouquet she will soon be carrying. A stiff ruff of tulle furthers the illusion, as do also the full ribbon bow and long streamers directed toward the guest-of-honor's place.

The bouquet of roses, feverfew, and delicate fern fronds was assembled in the hand, wrapped with green florists' wire to keep all stems in place, then encircled with gathered tulle.

A footed glass bowl container that resembles a very large champagne glass is well chosen for so festive an occasion as a bridal shower.

Tables that welcome springtime

Spring's the season to give a party! The budding branches, flowering shrubs, and jewel-toned tulips, daffodils, and hyacinths inspire you to set memorable tables, just because they're symbolic of the marvel of renewed life.

Take a hint from nature's designs when you plan flower decorations for the table. Display slender branches high or at the edges of your composition. Silhouette them, after careful pruning, to outline the beauty of every twig and stem. Then place masses of bloom low, for dramatic contrast and color impact.

Select containers that are simple and sturdy in character. These spring beauties are at their best in informal arrangements, in harmony with pottery or earthenware containers keyed in color to informal tableware or linens.

If your spring centerpiece is to include woody branches, guard against wilt by preparing ahead of time: pound stem ends and condition in deep water for several hours before arranging.

Create a landscape in miniature with a few branches of lilac, a few violets, and a bluebird.

Lilac branches should be pruned to take wanted outlines, then secured on a sturdy needle-point holder at one end of a shallow container.

The entire surface of the water is covered with floating violets and their foliage.

Cut short stems of the fullest purple lilac plumes you can find for this fragrant and colorful spring luncheon centerpiece.

Add white tulips to relate the flower design to its container and the tableware. Use a little fresh green foliage of both lilacs and tulips to fill in at the base.

Forsythia adds height and width to a centerpiece

All you'll need for this essence-of-springtime centerpiece are: three red tulips, four daffodils, and a half-dozen branch tips of forsythia, just coming to bloom. Cut stems short and include a little fresh foliage.

A round, footed bowl used as centerpiece is in harmony with the tableware, though not an identical match. And a handful of small pebbles disguises the needle point.

Spring gives us soft pastels

For fresh-looking centerpieces with that breath-of-spring air, concentrate on the pastel palette of bloom. Take advantage of the fragrant array in garden and florist shops at this time of year. On the table, it's like spilled sunshine, welcoming your guests to the teas, luncheons, and dinner parties of this hospitable season.

The pale blues, yellows, lavenders, and pinks that are so abundant among spring's flowering bulbs, branches, and trees will be harmonious in almost every decorating scheme. And these obliging colors also blend well with each other, when you want a mixed arrangement of spring flowers.

If you need height and drama in a table arrangement, look to the flowering shrubs and trees—crab, plum, pear, almond, cherry, quince, and many more. Their graceful branches will supply the tall, sweeping lines you want. Place the arrangement at one end of the table, and push it against a dining room wall to supply a background for silhouetted branches.

A circle of pansies, each face turned up so we can appreciate its charming features, surrounds a lifelike ceramic bird who appears to be much impressed with the solid bed of bloom beneath his perch. Placed on a coffee table, guests will look down into flower faces, appreciate the living poem to spring. Or use the arrangement as a centerpiece, on a dining table.

Stems were cut short and pansies massed in a shallow bowl. A similar effect could have been achieved with a posy-ring container—a shallow circle of glass or pottery—especially designed for easy display of flowers with short stems.

With flowering branches, you can afford to break rules concerning height. Here, tallest branch is about 3 times the length of the container, instead of the conventional 1½ or 2 times the length that is usually suggested. Delicacy of line avoids top-heaviness.

Red-leafed plum (*Prunus pissardii*) is the flowering branch used for this tea table arrangement, but quince or cherry would serve as well. Prune to get triangular form.

With the plum, we've used two early double and three single tulips, together with seven narcissus and seven golden daffodils.

Oriental arrangement of iris in an "East Wind" bowl achieves harmony between flowers, their style of arranging, and the container in which they are displayed. This design is of Dutch iris, but the bearded iris varieties can be similarly arranged.

Flower colors, chosen for their relation to the muted blues and lavenders of a luncheon cloth, are fresh and springlike, adaptable to a number of color schemes: imagine them on a yellow cloth, a green one, or as the only color in an all-white setting.

Seek a symphony
of colors in
the flowers you combine
with linens and
china on spring tables

Delicate hues of these flowers for the table hint of bridal showers and spring festivities. The arrangement is simple to focus full attention on the lovely color harmony. Darkest iris is used as a focal point, with a few iris leaves as accents, reflecting the leaf pattern of the chinaware.

Since this arrangement is constructed for front viewing only, it will be most attractive placed against a wall of harmonizing color, or at one end of your dining table.

Summer ornaments for outdoor tables

The charm of informality and warm summer weather are made for each other. Relaxed living and meals frequently eaten out of doors appeal to everyone. But just because dinner's served on the terrace or patio instead of in the dining room is no reason to forego the pleasure that flowers on the table bring to any meal.

To reflect summer's carefree mood, style the flowers for the table with informality. Use a mixture of whatever's most available in your July and August garden; or limit your arrange-ment to green foliage only. It will have a re-markably cooling influence on a warm evening.

Use durable flowers and foliage for your hot weather arrangements—those that don't wilt too easily. Nothing's less appealing on a warm day than the sight of a drooping bouquet.

Be informal, too, in your choice of container. Now's the time to try out a casserole, bean pot or mixing bowl as a flower holder. If it will match or contrast pleasingly with tableware and informal linens, by all means use it.

Picnic on the lawn (right) seems a real event when the table is decked with two bouquets of garden flowers in copper casseroles.

Echoing the vari-colored stripes of a simple runner that substitutes for a tablecloth, the twin bouquets are a grand and glorious mixture of anything and everything from the cutting garden. Spikes of green and white ribbon grass make a good foliage accompaniment to flowers.

Glass top table (opposite) in a frosty blue inspired this freely flowing table arrangement in shades of pink, magenta, and purple.

Clipped from a summer border, it includes: zinnias, phlox, rosy loosestrife for height, and trailing stems of petunias.

Create your own "gardener's choice" arrangement to imitate summer's generous temperament and ornament an outdoor meal.

The cooling greens (below) refresh a supper table on a patio that overlooks the garden.

Papyrus plumes, slender arrowhead leaves are intended to call up an image of lake or pond, reinforced by the decoy duck and some water-smoothed stones.

The simplicity of the two-color scheme in which the entire plan is carried out contributes to the restful, inviting atmosphere in this setting for an outdoor table designed by Mildred Brooks and Carmen Edgar.

Refreshing ideas for summer evenings

Pastels are fine for summer, but so are brilliant hues. Nature furnishes us with the hot reds, pinks and golds of zinnias, cockscomb, asters, geraniums, marigolds, nasturtiums, and a host of others which are at their best when temperatures are highest.

Take another hint from nature and cool off those vivid flower colors with fresh green foliage.

The crisp freshness of a black, white, and red color scheme is perennially cheerful and inviting. And it is especially well suited to the simple lines of contemporary tableware such as that used to set this patio buffet table for a summer supper party.

The color scheme is faithfully carried out by the arrangement as well, with chalk-white daisies and a focal massing of red geraniums in a black container. A background line of foliage adds desirable height to the design.

Both the table setting and the flower arrangement were designed by Mrs. F. W. Pickworth.

An exotic look for a buffet table comes both from a highly unusual container—an elephant that once supported a lamp—and the richness of the gold, black, and coral-red color scheme.

To separate the elephant from the black tablecloth, he was set on a gold-sprayed metal trivet; touches of gold reappear in the candlesticks and tableware.

Black grapes were wired to the base as a pleasing transition between flowers and container. Setting and arrangement designed by Mrs. F. W. Pickworth.

Decorate a table with the finest bloom in your garden

Porch luncheon (below) with the garden for backdrop, offers the gardener an opportunity for a gentle boast in the form of a flower centerpiece that displays his most perfect blooms.

Here, short-stemmed begonias and rose foliage are arranged in two shallow, rectangular containers, separated by a cooling piece of glass sculpture.

Splash gold on autumn tables

When fall's first crisp days put you in a mood to entertain, use the season's finest flower for centerpieces.

Chrysanthemums, in their gorgeous tawny colors are the traditional flowers of fall. Choose them often to crown festive occasions. Vary the style of your arrangement, the type of chrysanthemum you select to suit the degree of formality or informality of the affair for which they're used.

If your garden offers only small pompon varieties, supplement them with a few big shaggy-headed beauties from the florist's shop. They'll lend importance to any arrangement.

Baroque candlesticks were converted to containers by fastening on glass bowls with florists' clay. They're sumptuously filled with big bronze chrysanthemums, flaming fall foliage.

For variety, the flowers were arranged in twin designs instead of a more conventional single centerpiece that usually decorates buffet tables.

Rich brocade cover made to fit the table exactly and decorated with gold tassels sets the scene for a formal Thanksgiving buffet.

Shallow black container (left) running down the center of a table furnishes dramatic background for a series of small chrysanthemum arrangements carried out in the stirring colors of Indian summer—perfect for a fall party.

If you'd like a container similar to this, order a tinsmith to make one for you in measurements proportionate to the size and shape of your dining table. Then give it several coats of black—or whatever color you prefer—paint.

Appealing as a Japanese print is a table setting (right) inspired by a length of fabric from a gorgeous obi (the cloth used in classic Japanese costumes as a cinch or wide decoration at the waistline of a woman's kimono).

Since the fabric is so elaborate, the flowers are purposely simple—spider chrysanthemums and delicate branches of lycopodium. Linen napkins pick up jewel colors of the obi fabric in a table setting designed by Mrs. Nelson Urban.

Flowers for those special fall dinner parties

The bird-of-paradise flower (below), also called strelitzia, is an exotic from the tropics, especially in keeping if you plan a dinner menu featuring foods from faraway places. Never a "bargain" at the florist shop, these flowers repay you for your initial expenditure by being wonderfully long-lasting.

Each flower head consists of several florets. As first florets fade, snip them off so the next ones will have room to open.

Make a few stems of bloom look like more by combining them with ti leaves and an artistic grouping of colorful autumn fruits.

When crisp evenings and the tangy smell of bonfires remind us that another summer is over, it's time to open a new season of entertaining with a dinner party.

To decorate the table, choose chrysanthemums, putting on their annual show of color, or autumn's delectable harvest of fruits.

Vary the size of your centerpiece according to the length of the table. The design (including candles, if they are used) should equal approximately one-third the table's length.

Bright gold and bronze chrysanthemums complement the turquoise dinnerware; a brass flower bowl and candlesticks harmonize with flatware and goblets.

Tall tapers match the white linen cloth—well chosen as a neutral background for a table set with as vivid colors as this one.

In arranging the centerpiece, care was taken to place stems so each guest would have a pleasant view, with some bloom seen in profile, some facing forward.

The Midas touch of chrysanthemums is dramatic against a scarlet cloth. Lacy branches of evergreen extend the basic design of the arrangement and introduce interesting contrasts of form and color.

Tapers that match the evergreen, and candlesticks in the chinaware pattern help unify a setting of vivid contrasts.

Candles always add atmosphere, but they contribute most when they are clearly related to other elements of the table setting.

Peppermint stick carnations and long stems of dusty green eucalyptus foliage, borne by a romantic cherub, decorate a table set for a Valentine Day party.

In a container as shallow as this one, use a circle of saturated foam to hold stems securely in a horizontal position, keep flowers and foliage fresh.

The appeal of the candy-striped flowers is sharpened by the strongly contrasting background of a red cloth and the chalk white of milk-glass tableware in a buffet setting designed by Mrs. F. W. Pickworth.

Pay homage to St. Valentine with flowers

A heart motif is carried out with a white wire footed base for short-stemmed pink roses. Arranged in a needle-point cupholder, there's a bud on top.

Legend tells us that on February 14, 271 A.D., the Emperor Claudius put to death a young priest named Valentine for having defied an edict forbidding weddings (the Emperor thought single men made better soldiers) by performing secret marriages.

The martyred Saint Valentine lived on in romantic hearts in all the centuries that followed, his memory honored in a variety of ways.

In the Middle Ages, his followers held that the day was sacred to the birds who, on that day, chose mates. In Victorian times, a custom grew up of sending love notes—"Valentines" —to a sweetheart. Many were solemn proposals of marriage.

Today we play a less serious hearts and flowers theme on St. Valentine's Day. But, be as sentimental as you like when you design flowers to decorate a party table in his honor.

Twelve red carnations look all the redder against the white of a milk-glass epergne—a contemporary copy of an old-fashioned piece. The Victorian air of the hobnailed glass con- tainer echoes the sentimentality we associate with St. Valentine's Day. An arrangement of this sort is suited to use as a centerpiece for the dining table or to decorate a buffet.

Set a pair of golden lovebirds in a bower of pink roses to honor romance

A Valentine tea is a favorite occasion at which to announce an engagement. What better way to decorate a table than with our romantic centerpiece?

There are 13 blooms in this design, cut to different stem lengths and secured in a pair of needle-point holders.

To duplicate this arrange- ment, slant each rose so the bloom tips upward.

Salutes to nature's reawakening adorn tables at Eastertide

Apart from the religious ceremony of Easter, the season of the year in which it falls is one that people all over the world, from time immemorial, have celebrated. It marks winter's end, the joyful beginning of a new growing season.

It is this aspect of the holiday that we enjoy observing at flower-bedecked tables, dignified or whimsical in tone, depending on the occasion—family gathering, company dinner, or a children's breakfast to precede the Easter egg hunt.

Because the symbols of the season are so varied —bunnies, colored eggs, as well as flowers of springtime—there is a wide variety of themes to interpret in table settings. We show you two classic table arrangements, two inspired by time-honored myths designed to appeal to the young in heart or years. Let them stir your creative ability in setting tables to interpret spring.

Symmetry (above) in the flower arrangement befits a quiet dignity with which this dinner table has been set for Easter guests.

Tulips and lilacs seem to glow with color because they are set against an entirely neutral background—clear crystal goblets, gray linen cloth and napkins, and white china, delicately patterned.

At mid-day Easter dinner, you wouldn't use the candles.

Breakfast setting (left) to start off the day of the big Easter egg hunt would delight the younger set.

Handfuls of spring bloom in three little milk-glass containers are cheerful against a checked tablecloth in pastel shades.

Individual covered dishes in the shape of Easter bunnies—to hold scrambled eggs or hot cereal—plus a sprig of flowering almond laid on each person's plate are nice extras to please the young.

A carpet of spring bloom under a make-believe Easter-egg tree fashions a charming centerpiece for any informal meal at the Easter season. The children would enjoy helping to assemble it.

The short-stemmed flowers and a stark branch were secured in a cupholder and set onto a polished burl base to give the composition visual balance.

Colored eggs were pierced top and bottom and threaded with cord so they could be hung from the branches of the "tree."

Set your table to reflect the joyful season
of Easter, with flower arrangements that will create
a pleasant atmosphere for your family and guests

Inviting, tranquil appearance of this Easter Sunday table is due in part to the opulent color scheme—carried out entirely in gold and white.

Calla lilies, symbol of the season, are arranged simply in a low brass bowl, accompanied only by a few of their own green leaves.

White of lilies reappears in the tapers and in the elegantly classic gold-banded china.

Fruit and flowers celebrate Thanksgiving

Using the bounty of fall to decorate our dining tables is never more thoroughly in keeping with the spirit of the occasion than at Thanksgiving.

Fruit, especially, is a reminder of the reason for the first Thanksgiving, when our Pilgrim forefathers expressed thanks for a rich harvest season.

Pale green grapes, spilled lavishly forth from a simple straw cornucopia look twice as luscious for their deep purple background. On a green cloth, use purple grapes to obtain a similarly appealing color contrast.

Treasured silver (right) shows off the season's harvest of fruits in regal style. Arranged in a beautiful silver fruit basket, there's a richness about the grouping which matches the fine crystal, embroidered linen, and china used with it.

In colonial days, no flowers were ever used to decorate dining tables—only fruits. You'll be in the spirit of the first Thanksgiving if you choose to have a centerpiece of fruit on a holiday table. Let grapes spill over the edges, and tuck in a few green leaves with the fruit for a sumptuous look.

A handsome decoy (left) centered in a low arrangement of pine branches, garden chrysanthemums, and colored autumn leaves is an appropriate decoration for Thanksgiving, particularly if the meat course is the bounty brought home by a hunter.

Anchor the flowers and pine tips on needle-point holders in shallow glass cups ringed around duck. Choose flower colors to contrast with tablecloth.

The gleam of candles (below) and glow of gold add sophistication to a centerpiece of mixed fruits.

This bowl and candelabra are one unit, but you could use a separate fruit dish and candelabra in similar fashion on your Thanksgiving table, at one end, or—kept low—as a centerpiece.

Arrangements of fruit always have greater appeal if you concentrate on relatively few colors; do not use a mixture which appears unplanned.

*Holiday buffet
setting in a red and
black scheme*

Old and new are happily paired in a buffet setting that stars freshly cut greens—pine and juniper—and the glow of carnations to flatter the modern tableware and serving pieces.

Table was designed by Mrs. F. W. Pickworth.

Replace red with white carnations, lay a white cloth for a New Year's Eve party.

Fresh flowers and greens at Christmastime

Of all the charming customs of Christmas, none is older or richer in tradition than the "hanging of the greens." Boughs of evergreen —those seemingly miraculous plants which stay alive in deepest winter—brought into the house are still expressions of man's faith, in this joyous season that another spring will come, new life reappear.

In our celebration of Christmas today, no decorations are more freshly appealing than greens. And they are infinitely versatile, lovely to look at whether used alone or combined with a few cut flowers or fashioned into a swag, trimmed with berries or fruit.

The ivy and the holly, the pine and the mistletoe are traditional favorites praised in song and verse. When you use them on your Christmas tables, you will be honoring the age-old symbols of good cheer shared with family and friends at holiday parties.

Gilded magnolia leaves, wired together to resemble flowers, trimmed with gold tree ornaments festoon a swag created from feathery, long-needled evergreen sprigs to make a holiday centerpiece. Two white pillar candles of different lengths complete the arrangement. Play safe by fireproofing the greenery.

*Perch a cascade of red carnations
and holly atop
an elegant candelabra*

Brilliant companion for fine silver used on a holiday table is a burst of red carnations, spilling over sprigs of variegated holly. A glass bowl, holding the water and a needle point on which flowers and foliage are secured, was anchored to the central candleholder with a sticker disk from the jeweler. Display this arrangement on tea or buffet table and add to the effect by setting clusters of carnations on serving dishes.

Chapter 5

Here's what it takes to win a prize

To create beauty, and to share with others one's personal grasp of its nature are the twin forces that motivate all true artists, including flower arrangers. Flower-show entries carried out in this spirit will enrich both the arranger and the viewer who comes to look and learn.

For the stimulus they have provided to so many women to create and to receive pleasure from viewing the tasteful flower designs of others, much credit is due the State Garden Clubs and their National Council. They have set standards of excellence for staging, exhibiting, and judging flower shows that are universally followed and respected.

When you want to enter an arrangement in a flower show, your first step is to secure a copy of the schedule and study it carefully. Select a class whose specifications are a challenge to your imagination. Then decide on the particular materials you will use.

Make several practice arrangements, trying each time to improve until you feel you have accomplished the most artistic flower design you are capable of executing.

Pay special attention to the stated limitations on kinds of plant materials as well as accessories, colors, containers, and backgrounds you are asked to use. If the schedule calls for twelve roses and you slip in one more to improve your design, your entry will necessarily be disqualified by the judges.

Learn from the work of accomplished arrangers, such as the designs pictured here. Opposite are the three top prize-winners in the most recent Sterling Bowl tournament, sponsored each year by the Jackson & Perkins Company, the 14 contestants selected from 115 talented arrangers nominated from 45 states.

Mrs. E. O. Barton, first-prize winner, combined the rose Polynesian Sunset with a twisted stem of elaeaganus and displayed her design in an oriental bronze container.

Second-prize winner, Mrs. John Tumminello, (lower right) arranged mixed varieties in a soaring line in a sphere-shaped container.

Mrs. Samuel Fields, third-prize winner, combined bloom and bent canes of the rose Bronze Masterpiece, in a shallow container.

Related textures of alabaster bowl and petals of apple blossom made this pyramidal design by Mrs. J. R. M. Wilson a prize winner. Clusters of apple blossom were tucked into a saturated foam base, pruned to attain perfection of form.

Victorian footed container sets the style for an elegant symmetrical arrangement of roses, carnations, hyacinths, chionodoxa, double asters, with accents of leather fern. It won the Founders' Gold Cup for Mrs. Lawrence Hynes.

Homage to tradition

When the show schedule calls for period arrangements, there is a double challenge to the entering flower arranger.

First, it is essential to be guided by the basic principles of design that govern all successful compositions, whether modern or traditional: balance, dominance, contrast, rhythm, proportion, scale.

Second, it is important to be faithful to the period portrayed. This may involve using only flowers and foliage that were available in a specific era. Or, depending on the schedule's stated limitations, it may permit selecting from more modern plants those that seem to be in the spirit of the age concerned. The container, too, should be an authentic one or an accurate reproduction of a period piece.

For an arrangement that re-creates some style of the past—just as for a contemporary arrangement—ultimate goals are beauty, simplicity, expression, harmony.

A Dresden figurine, a Victorian stand for the milk-glass bowl which serves as container are harmonious elements of the total composition by Mrs. W. D. Keith and Mrs. Murray Morse featuring flowering almond, azalea, and tulips.

"Craftsmanship" was the class in which a vertical arrangement of ranunculus, daisies, and forsythia won the red ribbon for Mrs. Paul Smithson. The two designs at right were in the same class at the Chicago World Flower & Garden Show.

An antique mortar filled with geraniums, candytuft, coleus, and pittosporum is accompanied by its pestle, placed on a braided rug, with a backdrop of brick wall. The design won a yellow ribbon for its arranger, Mrs. S. J. Sennott.

Antique candle mold serves as a container for a composition combining ranunculus, ivy, and swirls of forsythia with three yellow wax candles. Designed by Mrs. Helen Pepke and Mrs. Opal Schrader, it was awarded the blue ribbon.

For authenticity in period arrangements, study the prints and paintings of the past to learn the varieties of flowers, fruits, and foliages that were portrayed

Romantically Victorian in air is this profuse arrangement of forsythia, flowering peach, jonquils, daffodils, tulips, hyacinths, and viburnum designed by Mrs. Marguerite Bozarth. The container she has chosen, an antique Waterford glass compote, is perfectly suited to the style of the arrangement.

Like a painting by some Flemish master of the seventeenth century is this graceful arrangement of mixed flowers and fruits. The full bouquet includes iris, carnations, tulips, lilies, stock, and ivy, with luscious grapes and strawberries grouped at the base. The composition was designed by Mrs. T. L. Cooke.

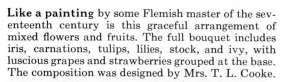

Originality is one of the goals that you will seek

Inspiration to use familiar materials in new ways is one of the valuable contributions a flower show makes to arrangers and viewers.

If you've gone along for years making more or less the same arrangements of roses, carnations or whatever your favorite flowers may be, attend a flower show and come away with fresh ideas on exciting new treatments for old and familiar flower friends of yours.

Better yet, *enter* a flower show as an effective stimulus to your creativity.

The flower designs pictured on these pages include a few exotic plant materials. But each has an air of originality because of the way material is assembled, or an unusual container. Each is the result of some inventive and creative thinking on the part of the designer.

When you enter a show, rest assured that if you take pleasure in creating a design, you've been rewarded, whether you win a prize or not.

Winter arrangement is of evergreen, dry artichoke heads and—for line—Strang weed (or pony tail). Mrs. A. B. Arrington chose a brown ceramic vase and a Japanese burl base to complete her composition.

An Ikenobo school arrangement of two tulips by Geraldine Thompson owes its appeal to the perceptive simplicity with which foliage and stems are placed, the attractive container, and the finish at the base given by smooth, dark pebbles.

Contemporary free-style Japanese arrangement by Lee Early Quinn is composed of two pieces of red torch ginger and a ti leaf held on a needle point in a handcrafted bowl of rough pebble texture. Design emphasized strong upright line. Polished pebbles were used to obscure the needle-point holder.

A swirl of locust pods with a tall branch of sour dock are the major ingredients of an arrangement which also includes a few fresh jonquils, a bird, and horse chestnuts filling the saucer container set on a straw mat.

It was a prizewinning entry in the Chicago World Flower and Garden Show by the Bensenville Garden Club.

Fragrant bloom of lavender, two artichokes and their curling foliage were combined with two hosta leaves in an arrangement by Marguerite Bozarth. Outlines of the base repeat curves of foliage.

Moss green vase lined in gray is related to green of hosta and gray of drying artichoke foliage.

Modern in manner is an artfully simple composition by Mrs. Jack Rardin. Curving lines are formed of foliage of *Sansevieria cylindrica* (tube-shape leaves).

Three heads of allium in an ascending line are placed in the exact center of the ceramic bowl that serves as a container.

Moribana arrangement of three stems of North Carolina black pine (with part of needles removed) is by Lee Early Quinn.

Inspired by Oriental styles of flower arranging, Mrs. A. B. Arrington designed this pleasing composition with two stems of Dutch iris and accompanying foliage combined with tendrils of elaeagnus.

Fuji chrysanthemums dried in silica gel, are the focal point of an arrangement by Mrs. Evan Lloyd which also includes glycerine-treated copper beech leaves, canna leaves, eucalyptus and locust pods and osage oranges at the base.

Holidays across the world was the class (for judges only) in which Mrs. Alfred R. Walpole won Blue Ribbon and Brown Ribbon awards with her porcelain drummer boy in a gold-backed niche arrangement featuring anthurium.

The warm glow of the floribunda rose "Spartan" is enhanced by its combination with copper beech leaves, driftwood, and two lifelike small birds. The arrangement was designed by Mrs. F. W. Pickworth, who used a footed container of pewter-washed copper and set it on a walnut base whose tones relate to driftwood.

Let the flower show schedule be your inspiration

The over-all theme of flower shows staged by member garden clubs of the National Council of State Garden Clubs is often related to the season. It is always chosen to help those entering find inspiration, and to lend the unity to exhibits that makes them rewarding to visitors.

As parts of the total show, each class within it is given a separate but related theme, and a set of specifications that will guide the entrants. This "schedule" may be quite detailed in requirements concerning: the type of exhibit; plant material to be used; color; container; accessories; size; theme; motif.

Conformance to schedule is a primary consideration in judging flower show entries, so it is important to study them thoroughly and to carry them out faithfully.

Craftsmanship was the class in which Mrs. R. O. Clark won a Red Ribbon for an old-fashioned mixed arrangement framed by a wood hoop, and grouped with a basket of rug wools, backed by coarse linen.

Another winner in "Craftsmanship" class at Chicago World Flower & Garden Show is Mrs. George Shambaugh's composition featuring a wheel, carved animal, swirling arrangement of spring bloom.

Blue ribbon in the same class as two designs at left went to Mrs. Harold Richie's composition symbolizing the craft of woodworking with tulips arranged in one end of an opened carved wooden chest.

A symphony in browns (right) is this all-dry material arrangement designed by Mrs. Merrill Cook.

Slim cattails give height; sorgo heads make the transition between deepest and palest tones, with dry yarrow heads as the focal point in the composition.

Adhering to colors of plant materials are an Ozark walnut compote used as container, and the base formed of two circles of walnut, one dark in tone, one light.

Azalea foliage showing fall coloring, combined with President Hoover roses in a brass water jug was a sweepstake winner in the classification "Textured Container." It was designed by Marguerite Bozarth.

The upward sweep of the azalea branches balances the handle on the water jug nicely, with a burl base effectively unifying the total composition.

Iris and spider, designed by Mrs. Harold D. Warren, combines all white flowers—iris, Solomon's seal, violets, mullein—with delicate fern fronds. The spider hangs from a thread and is watched by a frog who sits on a rock at the base of the arrangement in a porcelain bowl.

The artistic use of accessories

Many arrangers—particularly those to whom the modern and abstract styles are most congenial—often include sculpture, wood, stones, or "found art" of various kinds in their arrangements. They may do so to advance a theme, set a mood, or simply as a challenge to their skill in design.

If you are entering a flower show, you will, of course, include accessories only if they are permitted by the schedule.

In addition, you should be certain that any accessory you use, especially a piece of sculpture, has intrinsic merit. If it is of poor quality, it can only detract from the beauty you wish to create.

Driftwood of interesting form becomes part of this simple arrangement of lavender lupines displayed in a shallow pottery plate of lavender hue. Driftwood also serves a practical function by obscuring the needle-point holder. The arrangement was designed by Marguerite Bozarth.

Nature scene arrangement by the Timber Trails Garden Club of Elmhurst, seen at the Chicago World Flower & Garden Show, combines sprays of dried dill with fresh daisies and ranunculus for color. Two carved, stylized raccoons flank the lava rock base which is set in a bed of moss.

Acknowledgments

It is with great pleasure that we acknowledge our indebtedness to the many artist arrangers who have permitted us to photograph and to publish pictures of their designs in this book. They have, without exception, been most generous in their cooperation, happy to share with others the fruits of their experience, their special insights into the nature of beauty.

Colonial Williamsburg and its staff deserve our warm thanks for having supplied us with photographs of both living and dried plant materials arranged in authentic colonial style. We are especially indebted for the photographs that appear in this edition to Miss Marguerite Gignilliat of their Press Bureau, and to Miss Edna Pennell, Chief Arranger, whose work we show.

For allowing us to publish the excellent color photographs of the prizewinning entries in their Sterling Bowl Tournament, we are grateful to the Jackson & Perkins Company, as well as to the designers of the three arrangements we have included.

We appreciated very much the help of Helen Van Pelt Wilson who put us in touch with a number of the talented arrangers whose designs appear in the annual "Flower Arrangement Calendar" which she edits. And we thank the arrangers themselves who granted us permission to show examples of their work in this edition.

Finally, to garden clubs everywhere we express gratitude. Their officers have been unfailingly gracious in permitting us to photograph arrangements that were a part of the shows they regularly stage. It has, through the years, been a rewarding experience to be associated with them and their members.

Index